Jackie Warner

About the Author

MARTIN LEVY is a respected historical researcher
who has written biographical articles for the
Oxford University Press. He makes his home in
England.

Perennial

An Imprint of HarperCollins*Publishers*

LOVE
&
MADNESS

The MURDER of
MARTHA RAY, *Mistress*
of the FOURTH EARL *of*
SANDWICH

Martin Levy

A hardcover edition of this book was published in 2004 by William Morrow,
an imprint of HarperCollins Publishers.

FIRST PERENNIAL EDITION PUBLISHED 2005.

Book design by Shubhani Sarkar

The Library of Congress has catalogued the hardcover edition as follows:

Levy, M.J.
    Love & madness: the murder of Martha Ray, mistress of the Fourth
Earl of Sandwich/Martin Levy.
    p. cm.
    Includes bibliographical references.
    ISBN 0-06-055974-8
    1. Murder—England—History—18th century—Case studies.   2.
Ray, Martha, d. 1779.   3. Hackman, James, 1752–1779.   4. Sandwich,
John Montagu, 4th Earl of, 1718–1792.   5. Crimes of passion—
England—History—18th century—Case studies.   I. Title: Murder of
Martha Ray, mistress of the Fourth Earl of Sandwich.   II. Title.

HV6535.G72E545 2004
364.15'23'09421209033—dc21

2003056242

ISBN 0-06-055975-6 (pbk.)

05 06 07 08 09   RRD   10 9 8 7 6 5 4 3 2 1

TO JACKIE

To kill a rival is to kill a fool;
but the Goddess of our idolatry
may be a sacrifice worthy of the Gods.

WILLIAM HAZLITT

CONTENTS

Contents

ACKNOWLEDGMENTS

Love & Madness, unlike most short books, I believe, began life in one continent and grew to maturity in another. I first meditated a book about James Hackman's murder of Martha Ray in the summer of 1996. I was then living in South London, trying to make a living working part-time and spending a few evenings a week reading through a stack of eighteenth-century newspapers that a friend had given me. Late-eighteenth-century newspapers are full of strange and fascinating reports, yet the story of James Hackman's murder of Martha Ray jumped from the page. It clearly had some very unusual attributes. It wasn't just that Hackman was a clergyman and that Martha Ray was a singer and an earl's mistress; it was also the fact that the public of the time seemed extraordinarily moved by the murderer's predicament.

I finished the final version of the book in western New York in early 2003. Along the way, I accumulated a number of debts, to family, friends, a publisher and his readers, an agent, and an editor. In London Rachel Furlong offered the most encouragement. She listened to my ramblings after days and weeks spent in the British Library and made sure that I

visited the latest art exhibitions. In America my wife, Jackie
Warner, improved an early draft of the text in countless ways.
It is no exaggeration to say that without her, this book would
not have been published. Frances Kuffel, my agent at the
Maria Carvainis Agency, saw the book through to the con-
tract stage with HarperCollins USA, where Lyssa Keusch
edited it with exemplary patience. Raphael Kadushin of the
University of Wisconsin Press offered an enthusiastic vote
of approval. He very kindly sent the book to the late Roy
Porter, John Brewer, Maximillian E. Novak, Timothy Erwin,
and two other academic reviewers who chose to remain
anonymous. (Where I have not profited from their insightful
suggestions, I hope that they will attribute my failure to
incapacity rather than stubbornness.) For permission to publish material in the Sandwich Papers at Mapperton I must
thank the present Earl of Sandwich as custodian of the Earl of
Sandwich 1943 Settlement. The fourth earl of Sandwich's letter to Lord Loudoun in chapter 2 is reproduced by permission
of the Huntington Library, San Marino, California, and the
quotations from James Boswell's journals are published by
permission of Yale University Press.

A NOTE ON THE TITLE

Specialists in late-eighteenth-century English literature will recognize the title of my book as also that of a bestselling novel of the period. Herbert Croft's *Love and Madness: A Story too True. In a Series of Letters between Parties, whose Names would perhaps be mentioned, were they less known, or less lamented* took Martha Ray and James Hackman out of the magazines and newspapers, out of daily life, so to speak, and turned their story into a compelling work of literature. Croft's novel, first published in 1780, is worth reading alongside the short novels of Sterne, Mackenzie, and Goldsmith. Yet, there is no Penguin or Oxford edition of *Love and Madness*. Indeed, outside of a few academic departments, it is almost as if it never existed. Here I would like to acknowledge my debt to Croft in the matter of my title. I hope that his shade will forgive me for making use of it.

LOVE
&
MADNESS

ONE

Why Vainly Seek to Flee? Love Will Pursue You.

Martha Ray had a great deal on her mind during the evening of Wednesday, April 7, 1779, as her personal maid set about preparing her for a night at Covent Garden Theatre. She had not been out of the Admiralty building for several days, and as the mistress of one of George III's most hated ministers, the first lord of the Admiralty, John Montagu, fourth earl of Sandwich, she had good reason to worry about her security.[1] Many people held the earl personally responsible for the country's difficulties in its lackluster campaign against the rebellious American colonies and for the fractious behavior of its naval officers. Although news had recently arrived in London of a British victory in the southern states, many of the king's subjects were unimpressed. They had heard it all before—wild optimism, followed by retreat or surrender.

For several nights, gangs of roughnecks had taunted Sandwich and his mistress by singing antigovernment ballads under the Admiralty's back windows.[2] To the household, their behavior must have recalled recent memories of the night of February 11, when the Admiralty had been attacked by a mob inspired by a court martial's acquittal of one of Sandwich's enemies, the member of parliament and admiral Augustus Keppel. On that occasion, the mob had torn the courtyard gates off their hinges and broken most of the Admiralty's windows.[3] According to gossip Horace Walpole, Lord Sandwich, "exceedingly terrified," had fled with Miss Ray through the Admiralty garden to the Horse Guards nearby, where he had betrayed a "most manifest panic."[4]

Martha was about thirty-four years old; Sandwich, sixty. She was five feet five inches tall, dark-haired, and "fresh-coloured," with a cleft chin, bright, smiling eyes, and a warm, open countenance.[5] On this evening, her maid piled her hair fashionably high, dressed her in an expensively cut silk gown, ruched and lightly decorated, and finished by adorning her with a diamond cross and earrings.[6]

It was Sandwich who persuaded her to go to the theater.[7] He had much to occupy him at home. The opposition, led by the aristocratic and ineffective marquess of Rockingham and the epicurean Charles James Fox, had tabled another of several motions to inquire into his handling of naval affairs, and he had a speech to write and papers to assemble in his defense. As first lord of the Admiralty, his responsibilities included almost every detail of naval organization, from the inspection of George III's dockyards to matters of tactics and strategy.

Martha's heavy, four-wheeled carriage began the short journey to Covent Garden Theatre just after six o'clock.

Although it was early spring, an unusual warm spell enveloped London and green tufts of grass sprouted between the paving stones. Due to the Easter holidays, most of the capital's wealthier residents had already departed for their country estates or the spa towns of Bristol or Bath. Consequently, much of the traffic Martha passed was ordinary Londoners and foreigners, who lacked cooking facilities and were headed to the eating houses that thrived during this hour.

Soot blackened most of the buildings Martha's carriage rolled by, for London was a prodigiously dirty city with an unenviable reputation for ruining the health of its inhabitants. Traveling along Whitehall and into Charing Cross, her carriage took her through Cockspur Street and into the Haymarket and James Street. It then stopped outside a lodging house to pick up one of Martha's friends, a middle-aged Italian woman named Caterina Galli.[8]

Soon the two women passed along some of London's liveliest streets—probably Chandos Street and Henrietta Street, possibly New Street or Maiden Lane—the locations of innumerable acts of braggadocio and uncountable numbers of brothels, cheap lodging houses, taverns, and coffeehouses. They then traveled by Covent Garden's popular fruit and vegetable market toward the northeastern end of Inigo Jones's once fashionable piazza, where the carriage stopped and the two women alighted. They now stood outside the entrance to Covent Garden Theatre, one of London's three patent theaters. On either side of the doorway two guardsmen stood stiffly at attention as the ladies entered the building, gliding into a dimly lit lobby area crowded with a large and noisy gathering of fashionable beaux, fruit women, procurers, soldiers on furlough, and well-dressed ladies. Before long, Martha fell into deep conversation with a rakish young nobleman, an Irish beau named Lord Coleraine.

As the time for the play drew near, Coleraine escorted Martha and her companion into the theater and joined them for the evening. This night's entertainment was a benefit, one of a large number of performances set apart toward the end of each theatrical season in which the profits went to an actor or other member of the theatrical community. On this occasion Martha and others had purchased their tickets on the behalf of the singer and actress Mrs. Margaret Kennedy at the lady's lodgings in nearby Bow Street. Martha or Sandwich had paid dearly for the privilege, for Martha and her friends occupied some of the most expensive seating, one of the small number of stage boxes positioned immediately to the left and right of the stage and in full view of the rambunctious audience. It was here, too, that the king and other members of the royal family customarily sat; the king preferred Covent Garden to its rival at Drury Lane, partly because the latter theater was increasingly associated with opposition politics.

When the musicians filed into the orchestral well and the violinists began drawing their bows against their instruments' strings, a huge cheer arose from the upper gallery, which was reserved for servants and penny-pinching theatergoers and where seats cost one shilling. As was customary, they hurled orange peels into the pit area and onto the stage. Martha would have watched this element of the performance with equanimity, for it was a tradition common to all English theaters, and by no means a criticism of the fare or a slight aimed at particular individuals. Perhaps she was gossiping or signaling to friends. The interior was kept brightly lit for the simple reason that theater attendance was not merely about seeing the play. It was an intensely social activity with a great deal of sophisticated fan play and much peering through gentlemen's eyeglasses.

A bell rang to signal the rise of the curtain and the beginning of the performance. The orchestral music ceased and one of the company stepped through a stage door to recite a short prologue. Although this hasn't survived, the actor probably delivered a deftly worded piece, complimenting the audience on their percipience and generosity.

The green curtain then ascended to reveal a smartly painted interior scene of a cottage. The first play of the evening was an adaptation of a French comic opera on the old theme of frustrated but ultimately triumphant love. Called *Rose and Colin,* it was a slight piece of just one act, with five lively but barely delineated characters. There was little in the way of stage furniture—a table, a couple of chairs, a spinning wheel, some skeins of flax, a saddle and a bridle, a cushion and some bobbins for lace making. Presumably Mrs. Kennedy chose the play and its scant props to show herself off to best advantage.

Singing of one kind or another featured in almost every part of the evening. After *Rose and Colin,* Mrs. Kennedy presented another comic opera, this time in three acts, a performance of Isaac Bickerstaffe's ever popular *Love in a Village,* followed by the two-act pantomime *The Touchstone,* both of which were sprinkled with entr'acte entertainments. By the time the prompter's bell rang as the last curtain dropped, Martha was in all probability exhausted, for she had been in the theater for almost five hours.

She and her party emerged back into the lobby area just

after eleven o'clock. Moving slowly through the crowd, they headed toward the exit. Once outside and under the piazza, they were overwhelmed by the cries and curses of linkboys, livery servants, and hackney coachmen. Not the least of Martha's problems now was to find her coach amid the traffic jam. Coachmen who had parked their carriages nearest to the theater refused to leave until they found their employers, and so the carriageway locked at a standstill. Overhead, crude oil lamps suspended from the arches of the piazza provided minimal artificial light, as did the carriage lamps and the flambeaux carried by the linkboys. Now Lord Coleraine ungallantly departed, leaving Martha and Signora Galli to find their own way.

Fortunately, a young lawyer named John M'Namara, having some little acquaintance with Miss Ray, noted the ladies' distress and took the trouble to help them. He caught their coachman's eye and waited with them while the carriage plodded through the congestion. When the vehicle arrived, he handed Signora Galli into her seat and was helping Miss Ray toward the carriage steps when a man dressed in a black clergyman's suit suddenly rushed out of the shadows. Tugging Miss Ray by the back of her gown, he lifted his right hand and fired a pistol at her head. A split second later, he raised another pistol and fired it at himself. The force of this second shot knocked him to one side, and he fell to the ground. "Oh! Kill me! Kill me! For God's sake kill me!" he shouted, as he beat himself violently with the butt ends of both pistols.[9]

Possibly M'Namara's face was the last that Martha Ray ever saw, for though she had instinctively raised her hand as the clergyman pulled at her gown, there was little that she

Martha Ray. Engraving, undated, by an unknown artist after a portrait by Nathaniel Dance. A striking neobaroque engraving of Martha accompanied by a depiction of her murder.

could do to avert the catastrophe. With terrible finality, the bullet had gone straight through the side of her head. She was probably dead before she struck the pavement. The bullet wound was not the end of her injuries, however. The impact of the stone against her head caused a terrible contusion, making her bleed even more.

For a few seconds, no one knew what had happened. To M'Namara, Miss Ray could have fainted. He didn't realize the enormity of the violence until he noticed blood on his fingers. Hearing the report of the first pistol, he initially thought that it had been fired elsewhere, perhaps "out of wantonness," and only when he connected the blood with the ball, which had reverberated upon his arm, did he understand that Miss Ray had been brutally murdered.[10] The realization must have hit M'Namara with a stunning blow.

A local apothecary named James Mahon took charge by rushing forward and wrenching the pistols away from the murderer, who was now covered in blood, his black suit and hair sticky to the touch. The first screams went up and several bystanders raced to the scene, drawn by the age-old cry of "Murder! Murder!" The growing crowd around the corpse enticed other onlookers, and several people shouted excitedly when they realized that the victim was the mistress of the first lord of the Admiralty, and that the assassin was a clergyman. Determined to assess the extent of the assailant's injuries, Mahon ordered a constable to take the man to his Bow Street house, about eighty yards or so away. The clergyman made no attempt to escape. At times he swooned and the constable, holding him tightly, dragged him along.

Recovering himself, M'Namara and a linkboy carried Martha's body into a public room at the nearby Shakespeare's

Head Tavern. Immediately adjacent to the theater's entrance, the building was full of playgoers and actors. Now it presented a scene of disorder as patrons jostled with one another to view the dead woman.

Meanwhile, the constable—in spite of his best efforts—failed to attract the notice of Mahon's servants and was unable to gain entrance to the apothecary's home. He carried the wounded man to a local pub, but either the owner or the patrons refused them admittance. Someone then called him to bring the clergyman to the Shakespeare's Head, where Martha's body lay and where he could be properly secured. Once they arrived, M'Namara questioned the clergyman with a shaking voice: what could have possessed him to have committed such an act? The clergyman made no reply. Instead, he gave his name, James Hackman, asked to see Miss Ray, and requested that his brother-in-law be sent for. Apparently, he did not realize that Miss Ray was dead.[11] Someone searched his pockets and discovered two letters, one addressed to his brother-in-law, Frederick Booth, the other to Miss Ray at the Admiralty.

A solicitor by profession, Booth had been married to Hackman's sister for only five weeks and residing in their Craven Street house for less than a fortnight. He had been a close friend of the clergyman for several years and had often helped him by lending him small amounts of money.[12] Earlier that afternoon he and his wife had dined and taken tea with Hackman in the parlor of their home. For both Booth and his wife, Mary, the following two weeks would be a time of great stress and consternation. When Booth arrived at the Shakespeare's Head some minutes later, someone put the letter Hackman had addressed to him into his hands. He then opened it as Mahon leaned over his shoulder. Apparently

Hackman had composed it in a coffeehouse some three or four hours earlier, while Martha was in the theater. It appeared to be a suicide note.

> *My dear Frederick,*
>
> When this reaches you I shall be no more, but do not let my unhappy fate distress you too much; I have strove against it as long as possible, but it now overpowers me. You well know where my affections were placed; my having by some means or other lost her's (an idea which I could not support) has driven me to madness. The world will condemn me, but your good heart will pity me. God bless you my dear Fred. Would I had a sum to leave you, to convince you of my great regard: you was my only friend. I have hid one circumstance from you, which gives me great pain. I owe Knight, of Gosport, 100l. for which he has the writings of my houses; but I hope in God, when they are sold, and all other matters collected, there will be nearly enough to settle our account. May Almighty God bless you and yours with comfort and happiness; and may you ever be a stranger to the pangs I now feel. May heaven protect my beloved woman, and forgive this act, which alone could relieve me from a world of misery I have long endured. Oh! if it should ever be in your power to do her any act of friendship, remember your faithful friend,
>
> *J. Hackman.*[13]

Later this letter would be produced in court as evidence that the writer did not intend to kill Martha Ray, but to commit suicide.

In the meantime, while arrangements were made to move Miss Ray's corpse into a private room, messengers were dispatched to Sir John Fielding, Westminster's chief magistrate, and to Lord Sandwich at the Admiralty. Fielding, who had often met Miss Ray in his dealings with Lord Sandwich, was not in his Covent Garden office at the time of the murder but was quickly traced to his estate near Chelsea at Brompton. A scrupulous and public-spirited man, he had for more than thirty years been the mainstay of London's law, a guiding light by which successive ministers could navigate. Working at first with his half-brother, the novelist Henry Fielding (his predecessor as chief magistrate), then with his deputy, Saunders Welch, he had turned Westminster's magistracy into a beacon of relative incorruptibility. He was expert at finding new ways of catching crooks, and he possessed an entrepreneur's flair. No detail was too meager, no sensible idea too difficult for the tall blind man with the "little switch" and the black eye bandage to contemplate.[14] He also had a genius for publicity—he was, for instance, the first magistrate to make effective use of the press in pursuit of criminals. Such was his unique knowledge of human affairs that, according to one rumor, he could recognize more than three thousand thieves just by their voices.

Working under Sir John and operating from his private house and public office in Bow Street were the eighty or so Westminster constables, one of whom was Richard Blandy, Hackman's first official custodian. Appointed annually by the Westminster Court Leet—part of the city's administration—these men were part-time and unpaid, neither of which did much for their efficiency or for their reputation. Their incentive was the prospect of obtaining a reward, either in cash or in kind (sometimes they were rewarded with a "Tyburn ticket," a document that released them from any further duties within the parish or ward wherein the captured criminal had committed his felony). Doubtless Blandy already expected something from the earl, a few pounds, perhaps, as a testament of his gratitude. Beneath the constables were the watchmen. Fielding also employed a small number of paid detectives who worked full-time. The precursors of Sir Robert Peel's metropolitan police force, these were the so-called Bow Street Runners.

Back at the Admiralty, Sandwich had just gone to bed when the messenger arrived from the Shakespeare's Head. It was left to his elderly black servant, James, to break the news to him. Hearing a cacophony of voices outside the building, the earl first thought the noise issued from some ballad singers; it was only when another messenger arrived, this time accompanied by Mahon, that the servant was able to get the peer to understand that something terrible had happened to Martha. For a while, Sandwich stood petrified. Then, suddenly seizing a candle, he ran upstairs to his bedroom and threw himself onto his bed. It was not the first bereavement he had suffered in recent days, for just a week before his daughter-in-law, Lady Maria Hinchingbrooke, had died. Wringing his hands, he reportedly exclaimed, "I could have borne anything but this unmans me."[15] Calming himself, he then wrote a brief letter to the proprietor of the Shakespeare's Head, James Campbell, requesting that one of his servants might be allowed to sit up with the body and asking that steps be taken to prevent the prisoner from escaping. Amidst the flood of grief, he must have had some thought for the children he and Martha had had together—Robert, a midshipman in the navy; the schoolboy Basil, a future friend of Wordsworth, a radical lawyer and writer; the two youngest boys, William and John; and their daughter, Augusta, later the countess of Viry.[16]

Fielding arrived at about three o'clock in the morning, by which time Westminster's coroner, Thomas Prickard, had already impaneled a jury of twenty-four men for the inquest on Martha's body. Most of these jurors were local men, and Martha might have known some, such as the violinist John Abraham Fisher, who held a position in the orchestra at Covent Garden.[17]

Fielding requested two surgeons who were present to take off the top of her skull, a procedure that was later the object of much criticism for its seeming redundancy and lack of humanity. It was then discovered that Martha's injury was of a "very uncommon sort." "A full half of the *cranium* had been separated from the other, with a variety of ramifications of fracture from that part which immediately comprehended the receipt and discharge of the ball," the *Morning Chronicle* recorded. The ball came "against the *satura coronalis* which divides the *os frontis,* crossways, from the two *sagittal bones,* and pervaded its way to the *cerebrum*, &c. until it came out about half an inch beside the left ear."[18]

In the candlelit room, several jurors put questions to the surgeons. One particular "fat-bodied, pudding-headed" individual made something of a fool of himself when he insisted on asking Mahon for details of his conversation with Sandwich, "which surely," a writer to the *Morning Post* reported, "was not requisite for the inquest forming an opinion on the *deed*, and which he very prudently refused to answer." Fortunately, however, the "sensible part of the Jury soon put a stop

to these ill mannered, improper interrogations." Neverthe-
less, "upon the whole," the same correspondent added, the
inquiry still turned out to be the "most tedious and disgust-
ing" he had ever attended.[19]

Afterward, several witnesses gave their depositions,
including Mahon, two chairmen named John Glasgow and
Andrew Doyle, Mary Anderson, a fruit woman who had been
standing by the carriage, two constables, Blandy and
William Haliburton, and John Welsh, the watchman. No
account came from M'Namara, who, falling sick at the sight
of so much blood, had been allowed to go home. He would
give his deposition later.

The jurors were ready to conclude their inquiries some
hours later when daylight broke. Their verdict was death by
willful murder. After an interview with Sir John, the clergyman was committed to the bridewell at Tothill-Fields, near
Westminster Abbey. His legs were chained to a wall, and a
guard was set over him to prevent him from attempting suicide. "*What a change have a few hours made in me—had her
friends done as I wished them to do, this would never have happened,*" he said mysteriously, on his way to the bridewell.[20]

Remarkably, he then fell fast asleep.[21]

TWO

First Lady of the Admiralty

Martha Ray never talked about her early life. When curious acquaintances asked how she met the earl, she always changed the subject.[1] She might have felt that Sandwich's station demanded a mistress of equal or near-equal origins, and unable to provide antecedents even closely approaching his own, she said nothing. Nonetheless, some details about her early life became public knowledge after her death and were circulated in newspapers, magazines, and pamphlets.[2]

She was probably born in Covent Garden around 1745. Her father, Job Ray, had trained as a stay maker, while her mother, Mary, had worked as an upper servant in a nobleman's family. Together they opened a woolen draper's shop in Covent Garden's Tavistock Court about a year after Martha's birth, where their proximity to the Covent Garden and Drury Lane theaters must have made customers of actors and actresses. According to the *Town and Country Magazine*, Job was lazy and improvident. Although "esteemed a very good workman," he was "frequently arrested and involved in troubles." "This neglect of business, at a time, when he had a large family to support, naturally occasioned his wife to be displeased." In 1755 he moved out of Covent Garden to Holiwell Street, near the eastern end of the Strand, leaving Mary with control of the business.[3]

Mary then sent Martha to live with a wealthy aunt, who a year or so later, paid a premium to apprentice her to a mantua maker named Mrs. Silver of George's Court, St. John's Lane, close to the Smithfield cattle market. There Martha lived for about three years, working cheerfully at the tasks put before her, and was "generally spoken of as a faithful, diligent, and accomplished servant."[4] But if she felt destined for a life behind the counter, she was wrong. It was probably in St. James's Park that Sandwich first spied her, a sixteen-year-old girl lacking elegance but possessing self-confidence.[5] She was by no means a breathtaking beauty, but she was pretty, and anyway, Sandwich could hardly complain, considering his physical deficiencies.

As a tall, rather ungainly man, long-nosed and ashen-faced, Sandwich did not offer much in his appearance to attract Martha. His lopsided gait gave his friend Joseph Cradock the impression that he walked down both sides of London's streets at once. He himself used to quote the insulting words of his Parisian dancing master; apparently, this gentleman had once remarked that he would take it as a special favor if Sandwich did not reveal who had taught him to dance. Yet he had no trouble attracting women. Among his papers are letters from petitioners offering sex in exchange for

John, Earl of Sandwich. Engraving, c. 1780, by J. Corner.
A confident-looking Sandwich as he appeared on formal occasions.

favors, no doubt a nod to his social rank and office rather than to his own charms.[6]

Cultured and convivial, practical and unscrupulous, Sandwich was an aristocratic man of the world, methodical, intellectual, and profligate. To James Boswell he was a "jolly, hearty, lively man"; to the pious, a monster of self-indulgence.[7] During his years with Martha, he belonged to several gentlemen's clubs, including the Sublime Society of Beefsteaks, where singing formed part of the entertainment. The club met in a "handsome room" at the top of Covent Garden Theatre, on the ceiling of which was a gridiron. "We had nothing to eat but beefsteaks, and had wine and punch in plenty and freedom," wrote Boswell of his visit to the club in 1762. On that occasion Sandwich, acting as president, sat in a chair under a canopy. Above the peer, picked out in golden letters, was the club's motto: "Beef and Liberty," a palpable hit at the miserably fed French, governed by despots.[8]

The Society of Dilettanti was one club where Sandwich indulged his scholarly interests in art and archaeology. Founded as a drinking club in 1732, it sponsored expeditions to the ancient world, including Stuart and Revett's breathtaking exploration of Greece. Sandwich, who had traveled in Turkey and Egypt as a young man, encouraged the society to send an expedition to Lycia in Asia Minor in 1763. Through the society, he also helped foster the establishment (with Sir Joshua Reynolds as its first president) of the Royal Academy of Arts.[9] Yet there was more to the Dilettanti than art, archaeology, and drinking. Indeed the name of the society itself was something of a misnomer. Portraits of the members, for instance, are rife with political radicalism and sexual and religious innuendo.[10]

Like several other members of the society, Sandwich also played a leading role in the so-called Hell Fire Club or the Monks of Medmenham or the Order of St. Francis. Founded in the 1750s by his friend Sir Francis Dashwood, the politician, the club centered on a ruined Cistercian abbey on the Thames at Medmenham, near Marlow. Little is known in detail about the behavior of the monks except that they burlesqued the Catholic church and held orgies. The members "always meet in one general sett [*sic*] at meals," wrote the author of *Nocturnal Revels: or, the History of King's Place*, "where, for the improvement of mirth, pleasantry, and gaiety, every member is allowed to introduce a Lady of a chearful, lively disposition, to improve the general hilarity."[11] Some of the most suggestive details about the club are described in the notes to a poem by member John Wilkes; the inscription DO WHAT YOU WILL over the entrance to the abbey, a grotesque statue grasping his penis, an account of the younger monks' loves—all emphasizing the club's hedonistic qualities. Thus, the "garden, the grove, the orchard, the neighbouring woods, all spoke the loves and frailties of the younger monks," remarked Wilkes, "who [if they had sinned at all] seemed at least to have sinned *naturally*," which is to say, heterosexually.[12]

Later Wilkes fell out with Sandwich over politics. Ideologically, they occupied opposing camps. Like Sandwich, Wilkes was arrogant and opportunistic. He was charming and convivial, but his instincts were those of an agitator, and he lacked Sandwich's willingness to subordinate himself to authority. Since the summer of 1762 he had repeatedly attacked the government as pro-Scottish and anti-Whig, offering his own populist, "English" brand of politics. He had compared Scottish prime minister Lord Bute, George

III's favorite, to Edward II's rebellious and mighty subject Roger Mortimer, called the bishop of Gloucester's wife a prostitute, and intimated that the archbishop of Canterbury was a homosexual.

During the following autumn Sandwich entered the government's campaign to silence Wilkes. Appointed secretary of state for the Northern Department in the new Grenville ministry, he was to push through the prosecution. He did this with vigor, honing his attack with considerable guile, employing former friends of Wilkes as spies and informers. Determined to undermine Wilkes's public position by exposing his private character, Sandwich obtained a copy of an obscene and blasphemous parody of Pope's *Essay on Man,* and of the bishop of

John Wilkes. Engraving, undated, by J. Miller. Sandwich's onetime friend and political enemy.

Gloucester's learned notes, supposedly written by Wilkes and Thomas Potter. Bearing in mind his own licentious behavior, Sandwich surely should have avoided this direct approach, but somehow his political instincts failed him and, on November 16, he stood up in the Lords and recited it. Listening to the words of the poem, Dashwood (now Lord le Despenser) remarked, in mock horror, that it was the first time he had heard the Devil preach against sin.

By the end of the afternoon, Sandwich routed Wilkes,

but at the cost of his own reputation. Henceforth he was tarred with the name of "Jemmy Twitcher," the gangster who "peached" on his colleague Captain Macheath in John Gay's satirical *Beggar's Opera*. In other words, the rake was now a hypocrite.[13]

Politically, he had always been suspected of toadyism. During his early career he supported one of the great Whig magnates, the wealthy and irascible fourth duke of Bedford, a gifted man but negligent and incompetent. It was the daughter of one of Bedford's colleagues, an Irish peer, whom Sandwich married in 1741, raising speculation that political ambition had prompted the union. For several years the couple were happy, but then something drove them apart and she tottered into mental illness. Her friends blamed Sandwich for some unknown "Misfortunes" that had occurred in her family, while his enemies claimed that he mistreated her. It is unlikely that Sandwich was the most sensitive of husbands. In his private life, he could be arrogant and harsh, and not the least of his characteristics was a determination to put his own comfort before everything. In September 1751 he suggested that they both bury their complaints. If, he wrote her, they wanted outsiders to think that they got on well together, then they should actually do so. "I do declare that I still love You sincerely," he attested. But then, typical of his selfishness, he added that for him to be a dutiful husband, all she had to do was please him. In 1755 the couple separated. Sandwich remained at his country estate, Hinchingbrooke House, in the Huntingdonshire countryside, while Lady Sandwich moved into an apartment in Windsor Castle. Her health continued to deteriorate, however, and by 1765 she was living in a private madhouse, with "proper" management and servants.[14]

The failure of his marriage did not leave Sandwich too brokenhearted to pursue the teenaged Martha Ray. It is impossible to be certain how he approached her, whether he spoke to her in the park or ordered a servant to follow her. According to the *Town and Country Magazine*, he recruited Job Ray to act as his procurer; apparently, Job was overjoyed at the earl's interest in his daughter. It was, he remarked, *"the luckiest thing that could have happened."*[15]

Whatever the case, she did not make his way easy. Perhaps she had learned a lesson from her parents' unhappy liaison, for while he represented wealth, status, power, and sophistication, she refused to let him dominate her and she steeled herself to negotiate. After all, he was asking her to become his mistress, and though she had no experience of sex, she was practical and knew that even peers must pay for their pleasures. Importantly, she insisted on being treated exactly as if she were the real Lady Sandwich. Sandwich, with some qualifications, agreed. During the absence of his heir, the teenage Lord Hinchingbrooke, his country estate would, in effect, be hers. She would have servants, pin money, an equipage, and responsibilities.[16] He probably forgot to add that playing the role of Lady Sandwich required her to put up with his infidelities. Like many aristocrats, he was open-minded in his tastes. During their long relationship, he often sought the company of gentlewomen, as well as working girls and prostitutes. For many years he pursued Mary Fitzgerald, mother of "Fighting" Fitzgerald, the notorious bully and duelist, but his posturing failed to convince the lady. "Can't you be content that I do justice to your head, without persisting in wronging my judgment by supposing I want the very small degree of penetration necessary to see you are, and always have been acting a part? I own you an excellent actor: Garrick is not a much better," she wrote him.[17]

Despite the indignities of his disloyalties, their arrangement seems to have flourished, even though Sandwich's heir and his conventional neighbors naturally objected to what went on at Hinchingbrooke. Within a short time, Martha gave birth to their first child, Robert, and afterward, it is said, eight other children, five of whom survived her.[18] Meanwhile, Sandwich gave her with what was described as a "liberal education."[19] He engaged a succession of masters to teach her dancing, languages, and deportment. She learned how to play the harpsichord, and at some point her naturally beautiful singing voice was trained to a professional standard so that she could take the lead at Sandwich's famous Hinchingbrooke oratorios. The beginning of the oratorios is difficult to date, though they were established by 1759. Certainly there is no doubting their scale or their popularity. Generally, Sandwich set aside two whole weeks every year for the events, one during the summer, the other at Christmas. He expressed intense interest in the smallest details and insisted on a high level of organization.

"Every Oratorio, which was performed in the evening, was rehearsed throughout in the morning," wrote John Cooke, a clergyman friend of Sandwich's. "After dinner catches and glees went round with a spirit and effect never felt before, till everybody was summoned by a signal to the opening of the performance. This always lasted till supper was on the table; after which catches and glees were renewed with the same hilarity as in the earlier part of the day; and the principal singers generally retired to rest after a laborious exertion of about twelve hours."[20]

Sandwich invited some of the best professional perform-
ers in the country to these occasions. They included the
tenors Thomas Norris and Michael Leoni (on one occasion,
the Jewish Leoni offended his fellow Jews by singing in Handel's *Messiah*), the composer and instrumentalist Thomas
Greatorex, and the great composer and violinist Felice de
Giardini. By the late 1760s, Sandwich had placed the orches-
tras under the direction of keyboard player and orchestral
director Joah Bates, who had tutored one of his sons at King's
College, Cambridge, and who shared Sandwich's enthusiasm
for Handel. Usually Martha took the female leads. Her flat-
terers spoke of her as a second Saint Cecilia, but she was genuinely talented.

"Her Behaviour on those Occasions, on which for Six
Nights together, she alone supported the female Parts in different Oratorios and did the Honours of Ld. S's House to
every one's Satisfaction, was surprising and (if any thing)
might in some measure Apologize for his Attachment,"
wrote dramatist Richard Cumberland to his brother.[21]
Despite his "Attachment," Sandwich forbade his mistress to
speak to his female guests on equal terms. On one occasion,
an aristocratic lady tried to converse with Martha between
acts. Though she had not made the overture, Martha blushed
with embarrassment while Sandwich turned to a friend and
instructed him to tell the lady that "there is a boundary line
in my family, that I do not wish to see exceeded."[22] This double standard affected Martha in other ways. Invitations to
dine at Hinchingbrooke did not extend to ladies when
Martha was present, so that even long-married couples were separated at mealtimes. Naturally, Martha found herself even less
welcome outside of the house. She received an anonymous letter

from one of the Huntingdonshire "county" people complaining: "A Friend to propriety *desires* to caution Miss Ray *what* families she sends Lord Sandwiches servants to, *in her own name*, as it is very disagreeable to be obliged to remind those who forget themselves that their real situation precludes them from all intercourse with reputable families, where messages delivered *in her name* must be received with contempt by the very servants."[23] Another letter, this time addressed to Sandwich, upbraided the peer for allowing Martha to mingle among ladies, even without titles, in the stand at the Huntingdon races. Her presence there was an "insult," which should not be repeated.[24]

Some of Sandwich's female guests felt compassion for Martha. The wife of the bishop of Peterborough noted, "I was really hurt to sit opposite to her; to mark her discreet conduct, and yet to find it improper to notice her. She was so assiduous to please—was so very excellent, yet so unassuming! I was quite charmed with her; yet a seeming cruelty to her took off the pleasure of my evening."[25]

Hurt, Martha wisely developed strategies to cope with these reversals. The petty discomforts of her position at Hinchingbrooke kept her at Hampton much of the time, where Sandwich owned a villa and where a close neighbor was the distinguished actor David Garrick. At the Admiralty she often took a hand in entertaining Sandwich's wide circle of friends, which included politicians, senior naval officers, scientists, and philosophers. Doubtless she enjoyed the atmosphere of joie-de-vivre that surrounded these evenings, where whist followed coffee and where the conversation was instructive as well as entertaining. Denied intimacy with Sandwich's family and his female friends, she built up a network of mistresses, musicians, actors, and society people. One close friend, Kitty Walker, lived with Sandwich's military friend, the fourth earl of Loudoun, while another, the formidable Mary Ann Yates, earned her living as an actress and co-manager of the Haymarket Opera House. A third was Caterina Galli, the Italian woman who would accompany her to Covent Garden Theatre on that tragic night in April 1779. Sandwich had hired Galli, a retired vocalist and former pupil of Handel, to serve as a companion for Martha and to develop her voice. According to rumor, she had also been one of his mistresses.[26]

Admiralty.

 *Admiralty.* Engraving, undated, by J. Green after a painting by S. Wale. Martha lived at the Admiralty for much of the 1760s and 1770s.

The gentlemen Martha befriended were no less interesting. Some nights at Sandwich's dinner table, Martha found herself chatting with the naturalist Joseph Banks, with whom she shared a passion for birds, and Banks's colleague Captain James Cook, the eminent navigator and explorer. Thanks to Sandwich's patronage of Cook, during the summer of 1774 Martha was introduced to the celebrated Polynesian traveler Omai. A native of the Society Islands in the distant South Seas, Omai had arrived in England in July aboard Tobias Furneaux's ship the *Adventure,* following which he spent several weeks as a guest of Sandwich at Hinching-brooke. Canny and "prodigiously" liked, Omai impressed observers with his gentle manners and flirtatious ways. "He is well behaved, . . . and remarkably complaisant to the Ladies," remarked Sandwich's friend Dr. Daniel Solander.[27] Other commentators noticed how an enraptured public feted him. "The present *Lyon* of the Times, . . . is Omy, the Native of Otaheite," gasped novelist Fanny Burney in her diary.[28]

At Hinchingbrooke Sandwich treated Omai as an honored guest—though as a "savage" he must be trained; and day followed day in a round of "civilizing" influences. On one occasion, the peer took him boating upon Whittle-Sea Meer; on another, he treated the South Seas native to an oratorio. He even took Omai on a fox hunt. Like many Englishmen, Sandwich was surprised and fascinated by the Polynesian's nonchalance. The launch of a man-of-war at Woolwich failed to move him; the sight of Greenwich Hospital left him unimpressed. "If that did not surprise him nothing would," Sandwich remarked after the trip to Greenwich, "for that he never could have seen anything half so magnificent."[29] Some of Omai's remarks on his host's domestic arrangements suggest that he possessed a good deal of fashionable sentiment. When, toward the end of the Polynesian's stay in England, the reformer Granville Sharp attempted to convert him to

Christianity, Omai took a bundle of pens from the earnest man's desk and made the following point: "There lies Lord S——," he said of the first pen, "and there lies Miss W[ray]." Then, taking a third pen he placed it at a considerable distance from the others, "and there lie Lady S——, and cry!"[30]

Of course, life at the Admiralty, as at Hinchingbrooke, brought its own share of problems. At Martha's urging, Sandwich appointed one of her friends, a Mrs. Berkeley, housekeeper at the Navy Office. To some observers, the appointment looked like a quid pro quo for Martha's attachment to him. Sandwich's enemies accused her of exploiting her intimacy with the earl for financial gain and influence. When rumors surfaced that Mrs. Berkeley stole from the Admiralty, their accusations seemed justified.[31] Questions continued to be asked about Martha's honesty, and no wonder. Some of the letters she received were breathtakingly frank and must have tempted her. An anonymous lieutenant offered her four hundred pounds toward the purchase of a "piece of plate" if she would use her influence to engineer his promotion to the rank of master and commander. A "line directed to RL—Hamburg Coffeehouse Royal Exchange will be esteem'd a favor & the utmost secrecy observ'd," he added.[32] Martha was certainly willing to use her influence to forward careers, as evidenced when she saved from "total ruin" a "giddy young Man" presumably by providing him with money or an introduction. Knowing nothing of her murder, the grateful youth sent her a detailed account of his travels, from off the Cape of Good Hope, some three weeks after her death. He concluded his letter by appealing to her acquisitive instincts. "If there is any thing in the part of India we are going to, you wou'd chuse to be sent to England, I shoud think myself the happiest

Creature on Earth to be honour'd with any of your Commands," he told her.[33] Sandwich's opinion of anyone who attempted to bribe Martha was reputedly strict. When one of David Garrick's correspondents questioned him about the propriety of sending "Trifles" to Martha's children, Garrick told him that Sandwich "immediately abandons any person who thinks to make an Interest thro' that Channel."[34]

If she was open to bribes, it was the result of insecurity. The few letters that survive from Martha testify to the fact that even at the best of times she felt that her position was precarious. Sandwich often bullied her. He was unscrupulous and suspicious of her friends, and they argued heatedly about his rudeness and her extravagance. About money she could be cavalier. As a former mantua maker, she appreciated a good silk, and she was unable to resist a bargain. Like many Londoners, she was enchanted by the great variety of goods available in the capital's shops. Shopping was an art form as well as an enjoyment, and she was undoubtedly fond of her regular excursions to the Strand and Oxford Street, and even beyond. On one occasion, in Brussels, she laid out over two hundred and fifty pounds on linens and silks. Sandwich had warned his friend Sir William Gordon, the envoy, to keep a watch on his mistress's expenditure, but even this practiced diplomat's lectures proved futile. "Durand & myself did every thing in our Power to prevent Her laying out so much money in laces stockings caps gowns, etc. etc., knowing the difficulty she would have in introducing Them into England but our Remonstrances were ineffectual as she found Every thing such bargains—Indeed, how she will contrive to get ashore the Velvet and silk Coats which she destines for your Lordship I cannot conceive."[35]

They fought about the price of everything, from buckles to beer. Martha complained that the housekeeping money Sandwich allowed her was insufficient, and she resented having to dip into her pin money. Alone in London in the summer of 1766, she received an angry letter concerning a bill, which she had forwarded from their vintner. "I shall be very happy when this Housekeeping is at an end," she replied in her distinctively messy hand, "for it is both a grate care and trouble."[36] Such remarks sometimes give a petulant tone to her letters, as if, unsure of her situation, yet sure of her sexual attractions, she enjoyed playing on the much older man's financial insecurities. Although quick to assure him of her love—often ingratiatingly so—she never departed from the more formal modes of address, at least in her letters that survive. Even after ten years, her lord was still a lord. She was his "most affectionate M Ray," never the more familiar "Martha."[37]

Later that summer Sandwich discovered that she had approached the management of Covent Garden Theatre about the possibility of an engagement. He reacted with anger and disappointment, writing her a pained and searching letter. Martha did not deny her scheme, but she disputed that an engagement was imminent. But how else was she to make ends meet, if she did not resort to the stage? Had he himself not said that he would no longer pick up her debts for her? Her musical friends had assured her that she had a wonderful voice. Surely she would succeed on the stage. And besides herself, who else, bar him, did she have to rely on? She wanted him to be happy, but then, he had to make her happy, too. "I am not a slave, nor will I suffer myself to be treated as such, tho of late not much better," she informed him in one particularly virulent letter.[38]

Painted by N.Dance R.A. 1777.   Engrav'd by V.Green Mezzotinto Engraver to his Majesty, & to the Elector Palatine.

Miss Martha Ray,

who was MURDERED April 17.th 1779.

Published May 25.th by V.Green, N.º 29, Newman Street, Oxford Street; & at N.º 52, Strand.
Se vend à Londres, chez les Freres Torre, Marchands d'Estampes.

⊗ *Miss Martha Ray.* Engraving, 1779, by Valentine Green after a
portrait by Nathaniel Dance. Green based several other engravings of
Martha on Dance's portrait.

Sandwich reasoned that if she was looking for a means of support, she must be having an affair and preparing to leave him. In one letter, he intimated that he had been told she was pregnant. For this he received a brief lecture on trust. He should not listen to gossip. She was not pregnant but ill. "I never was guilty of what the world may lay to my charge," she told him.[39] With characteristic guile, he employed his friends to make discreet inquiries on his behalf. Having already sent the apothecary and surgeon Herbert Lawrence to interview John Beard, the manager of Covent Garden Theatre, he now dispatched his secretary, Richard Phelps, on the same errand. Like most aristocrats, Sandwich could depend on a good deal of inherited and acquired obligations, and he was not above using his minions to call in his advantages. Phelps reported his findings in minute detail. Beard, he wrote, had claimed "that he would never take her upon any account unless he knew that your inclination went along with it." Phelps assured Sandwich that Beard had been warned. Whatever Martha's intentions, her appearance on the stage was not to be. Beard assured Phelps that if he ever heard of her attempting to sing professionally, he would hasten to inform the secretary. Although, like Sandwich, Phelps quickly came to doubt the sincerity of Martha's threat, he added that she was "too clever not to know all her advantages," if such a resolution was taken.[40]

In the meantime, Sandwich did offer Martha some sort of compromise. Presumably he agreed to pay her bills. The details are obscure, but on the same day that Phelps composed his letter to Sandwich she wrote to the earl, expressing deep satisfaction with his offer. "I am much happyer then I ever was in my life, as I am quit[e] convinced your love for me, is such that I never culd leave behind," she assured him. Henceforth, "in returne for so many proofs of sincere love," she would devote herself heart and soul to his personal happiness. Phelps, she added, had made her life "happy for ever," for playing a leading role in forwarding their reconciliation. "Let me beg to hear from you as soon as possible," she added.[41]

This cheerful missive aside, Martha was, as she had written Sandwich earlier, ill. The sickness of which she had complained during the summer seems to have recurred, and during November Sandwich was sufficiently concerned to send an account of her condition to the eminent obstetrician and surgeon William Hunter. A hardworking and gifted anatomist, Hunter, was well versed in the afflictions of the elite, counting the queen no less among his list of wealthy and titled patients. Unfortunately, he was unable to diagnose the root of Martha's problem. She may be pregnant; she may not be, he told the worried earl. "Be that as it may if the Menses do not return I would have Miss Ray (if she can without fear) in the very beginning of the 8th week, that is, in a few days, be bled four or five ounces, and keep pretty quiet in body & mind at least for a month to come." Should she be pregnant, and should she miscarry, she was not to be alarmed. "Upon such occasions there is sometimes a good deal of pain, and often *apparently* dreadful discharges, but *never* real danger. Nature always finishes it with safety."[42]

These are not the only references to Martha's gynecological problems in her relationship with Sandwich. Many years later the earl again invited Hunter to comment on her condition. This time she was complaining of giddiness and loss of blood. In his letter Hunter wrote of "Obstructions left in

Parts" inflamed. He recommended gentle exercise and a "strengthening" medicine, "such as a Decoction or Infusion of the Bark twice or thrice a Day," and some special pills in case of costiveness. "Her Diet should be of solid Foods rather than slops, and should consist chiefly of white meats, plainly dressed, of flat Fish, shell-Fish and Rice, Barley, Sago, Roots and Greens that are in common Food." He also recommended ass's milk "as a Part of Food easily, in general, digested," and added that she should bathe the inflamed parts "Night and Morning with a Bladder half filled with Bran and warm Water, and wrapped up in a Flannel moistened with Brandy and Water, and afterwards [rub] the part long and powerfully with a little Oil."[43]

Whether Hunter's suggestions cured Martha's affliction or merely eased her symptoms is impossible to say. On neither occasion does he appear to have examined her. Possibly some of her health problems were exacerbated by feelings of insecurity. She often asked herself what would happen to her and her children if Sandwich should die. She knew she could not count on his heir to look after her.

During the summer of 1772 her fears in this respect were the ostensible cause of another blazing row. Having contradicted rumors put about by Sandwich's son that she would be debarred from Hinchingbrooke House for the duration of the Huntingdon races, she received an awkward letter from Sandwich confirming them. Blinded by fury, she wrote a sharp letter from London, reminding him of the terms under which she had first agreed to live with him, and recalling the several affronts she had received on his behalf. "You best know your motive for keeping this scheme a secret from me," she wrote, "but I cannot esteem it friendship." She offered the earl a fait accompli. "Since it is your pleasure to forbid me your House at the Race time, you'l pardon me if I desire in return to exclude [myself] from it on all other Occasions."[44] True to her word, four months later she was still in London. For a while Sandwich tolerated her absence, but with the approach of winter, he grew increasingly anxious over the fate of his oratorios. He begged her to come home. Martha responded with a masterpiece of subterfuge. Even if she did return to Hinchingbrooke, she was ill—far too ill to sing at his oratorios.[45]

Sandwich's side of their correspondence no longer exists, but it is clear that he was desperate not to lose her. On October 22 Martha responded to one of his letters with her bitterest outburst yet. Shifting the grounds of her resentment from Lord Hinchingbrooke and his attitude toward her and her children to the question of her future provision, she revived many old complaints and touched on several new ones. In his letter he had expressed surprise at her behavior toward him, but with what justice, she asked. Surely he had only to reflect upon his conduct toward her to realize that his treatment of her had been anything but affectionate. Few women, she complained, would put up with his insults while receiving nothing. She asked him to recall their conversation of a previous week, in which she had pressed him to reveal how she and her family were to be provided for. "Your reply was this[:] that I must trust entirely to you in that particular . . . that I had no right to mention these sort of things to you." Well then, if he refused to talk about money, she would not return to Hinchingbrooke.[46]

Resignedly, Sandwich wrote that day to his friend Lord Loudoun for advice. He suspected Loudoun's mistress, Kitty Walker, of adding fuel to their disagreements. Once more, he wondered if Martha had taken a lover. After all, he reasoned, she would not risk losing him unless she had someone waiting on the side. Perhaps, he now reluctantly concluded, they would have to part. After all, the question of any future provision was an absurdity. "The alteration in Miss Ray's behaviour for some months past has been such as is not easy to be described," he wrote. "She has been practising all the stale tricks that have been used against children for centuries past, & which never came into her head before; she has shewed a large catalogue of debts (unknown to me) which I shewed some disposition but have made no promise to pay except in part; & certainly shall not if she leaves me." Sandwich wrote that she had urged him to make her a settlement, an idea that had never occurred to her during their eleven years together. He accused Loudoun's mistress of putting this distasteful thought in her head. He added, "I will not conceal from you that nothing can be a greater calamity to me than the loss of Miss Ray, but as things stand at present unless you can interpose I see very little probability of preventing it; giving way to a woman in unreasonable points never does any good, besides I never did nor never will make a settlement, it is too foolish a proposition to tell the reasons against it."[47]

Before Loudoun had time to reply, Martha wrote to Sandwich again. She had a long way to go before she would weaken. In response to Sandwich's accusation of her "want of feeling," she answered, "Oh Lord Sandwich be assured the want of feeling is on your side."[48] In her next letter she expressed amazement at some of his assertions. If he imagined that she thought herself in error for anything that she had done, he should think again. She had merely asked him to show her his will; at no time had she mentioned a settlement. Once more, she reminded him that she was not without "spirit & proper resolution." She continued, "Depend on

one thing, that you shall never fright me into compliance let
the consequences be ever so bad to us both."[49] As during
their earlier row, Sandwich sent his friends to question
Martha on his behalf. One such errand boy was a Huntingdon neighbor, an army officer named Lawrence Reynolds. A
careful man, Reynolds must have impressed the earl with
his urbanity and tact, though for reasons that will sub-
sequently become clear, the choice was a richly ironic one.
Determined to appear fair-minded, Reynolds did not reveal
that he had been sent by the earl. Clearly he construed his
purpose as more consolatory than combative, and he did not
want to compromise his status as a disinterested neutral.[50]
For her part, Martha was impressed by the gravity of what he
had to say. Within days of their first meeting she was at last
prepared to compromise. Indeed, she went further than compromise, even conceding on the matter of the will. "I do give
you my word & honour that I never will mention a word on
that subject any more," she wrote on October 28, but then,
surely sarcastically, "I am now quit[e] convinced what I am to
trust to." Her surrender delighted Sandwich. As an added
bonus, he received her agreement to perform at his next
musical meeting. This concession was, however, hedged
around with reservations about her health. "Don't flatter
yourself that it is for my own pleasure," she wrote. "No
quit[e] the contrary. I shall do it to obey you."[51]

A few days later Sandwich received Lord Loudoun's reply
to his letter of October 22. In it, Loudoun urged Sandwich to
make Martha a settlement.

You say you never will give Miss Ray a settlement.
Think who she is a ripe woman whom you debauchd

very young who you tell me has lived with you eleven years. I see she still possesses your fondest wishes. She has brought you a fine family of children whom you seem as fond of as any father can be of children. From all I have seen in her conduct or could gather from her conversation I never could observe she had the least attachment or even thoughts of any other man and indeed from all I have ever heard. . . . I do not believe she ever was had by any other man but yourself.

Now my Lord consider with yourself that if you were to die what must be the situation of Miss Ray from that moment; she must be immediately in want of bread unless you give it to her. Miss Ray is a fine woman but she is not the same as when you brought her into this stile of life. You told me she is now twenty nine. She has had five children to you. I hope your L[ordshi]p will forgive me for saying you ought, not only for the love you bear her but for your own honour, instantly to put her into a situation to be out of want, if an accident were to happen to you tomorrow.[52]

Martha certainly didn't forget her financial concerns. One evening, shortly before her death, she asked Joseph Cradock if he would broach the subject of a settlement with Lord Sandwich upon her behalf. She appeared "much agitated," according to Cradock, "and at last said, 'she had a particular favour to ask of me.'" Cradock responded that no one but Martha herself could approach the earl with such a proposal.[53] Presumably Martha then let the subject drop. At least, there is no record that she again brought it up with Sandwich.

THREE

The Romantic Redcoat

Before entering the clergy, James Hackman forged a career in the army, and so it was not as a minister but as an ensign that he first met Martha. During the afternoon on December 16, 1773, Hackman, whose regiment was quartered about twenty-five miles from Huntingdon, was strolling by the gates of Hinchingbrooke House with another soldier, a neighbor of Sandwich's named Lawrence Reynolds. Sandwich happened to spot the two men and, recognizing Reynolds, he invited them to dine at the house. They accepted, and after dinner and coffee, someone suggested a game of whist. Hackman asked if he could watch rather than play, so Sandwich and Martha paired off against Reynolds and the writer Joseph Cradock. After the second game, Sandwich pled tiredness and a headache and retired early. He had had a long day, traveling twenty miles from Cambridge, where he had participated in an election for a new professor of chemistry at his old college, Trinity. Soon afterward, Martha retired, too, and the three men were left alone. Cradock, an astronomy enthusiast, suggested they assemble the new lunar telescope that the earl had just received from London. Hackman and Reynolds agreed. "Lord Sandwich's old black servant opened the box, and we remained upon the lawn till it was late, and possibly might return again to the table," Cradock remembered.[1]

In whatever way the evening ended, thereafter Hackman found numerous excuses to visit the earl's estate, watching for every opportunity to speak to Martha alone. Perhaps a significant word or look had passed between them at Sandwich's table. She must have seemed like a glamorous figure to him, sophisticated and cultured, even mysterious. If he was smitten then, he soon became obsessed, accompanying her on her morning rides in the Huntingdonshire countryside.[2] Perhaps she was his first love and the extremity of his emotion matched its novelty. For her part, Martha encouraged the younger man's passionate attentions, clearly flattered by his interest.[3]

James Hackman had the bravura of an attractive and complex man. About five feet nine inches tall and "very genteelly made," he impressed observers with his social poise and dignity.[4] He took pleasure in books of a scholarly nature and—what was much admired during the eighteenth century—the art of witty and intelligent conversation.[5] He cultivated his less serious side as well, for he was fond of plays and pleasure gardens and frequently visited Ranelagh and Vauxhall.[6] According to the *Town and Country Magazine*, he possessed a "good voice, and some taste for music," two qualifications that would most certainly have earned Martha's notice.[7] Yet there was also a physical side to his character that Martha might have found equally appealing.

Dighton del.   Laurie Sc.

THE REV^D. JAMES HACKMAN.
From the Original Drawing by Mr Dighton
Pub^d as the Act Directs May 18th 1779 by W. Richardson N° 68 High Holborn

The Reverend James Hackman. Engraving, 1779, by Robert Laurie
after a drawing by Richard Dighton. The young murderer as a man of
sentiment. COURTESY OF THE NATIONAL PORTRAIT GALLERY, LONDON

In his youth he had hunted with dogs, and he was a dexterous horseman.[8]

By the time of his birth in 1752 in Gosport, the Hackman family had lived in the coastal Hampshire town for over forty years. James's father, William, his uncle James, and their sister, Ann, were townspeople born and bred, having been baptized in the parish church, Holy Trinity. James's father and uncle became naval officers. By 1752, William had been a lieutenant for almost thirteen years, the highest rank he would ever achieve, and he died leaving little obvious impression on his contemporaries. The elder James, on the other hand, became a commander and then a captain and played an active role in the town's civic life. In 1763, along with fifty or so of Gosport's other residents, he was appointed trustee of an act for the better paving of the town's streets and for the "preventing" of countless "nuisances."[9] This seemingly ordinary piece of legislation was an important spur to the town's development. Not only did it signal a new, more forbidding attitude to unsanitary conditions, but it also gave the trustees the power to levy fines for persistent infringements.

To most observers, Gosport during this period was virtually uncivilized. Indeed, long after the act was put into force, the town remained a byword for filth, pettiness, and bigotry. "Gosport can claim little that is attractive; for the town is not pleasant and the surrounding country has no peculiar charms," wrote the Reverend Dr. James Bennett in 1777. "[It] has the narrowness and slander of a small country town, without its rural simplicity and with a full share of the vices of Portsmouth, polluted by the fortunes of sailors and the extravagances of harlots."[10] Since midcentury the town had been the site of a vast, purpose-built hospital, for sick and wounded seamen—reputedly the largest English brick building of its time and, in the words of a writer in the September 1751 *Gentleman's Magazine,* "a noble, strong, and beautiful fabric."[11] In the Gosport coffeehouses the talk was of French and Spanish fleets, the likelihood of "prizes," of squalls, of sailors' myths, of sudden wealth, and of the vicissitudes of governments. As a victualling center, Gosport was home to master brewers who supplied the navy with grog, while during wartime numerous enemy seamen were imprisoned there.

In 1750 William Hackman married a local girl named Mary Mathis. Nothing is known of their married life, except that Mary gave birth to James and to a daughter, Mary. Possibly, William had high ambitions for his young son. Sometime in the mid-1760s he sent him from Gosport to board at a school about fourteen miles away in the small town of Bishops Waltham. Run by a Mr. and Mrs. Gibson, the school emphasized the classics and math and catered to a handful of day boys and about thirty boarders.

One of James's contemporaries at the Gibsons' was the future composer and memoirist John Marsh. An almost exact contemporary of James, and like James the son of a naval officer, Marsh was a happy, confident child, who clearly enjoyed his time there. While he does not mention James by name in his account at the Gibsons', he does suggest that there would have been much for young Hackman to do there. Although the boys were worked hard at their books, ample time was allowed for recreation and enjoyment. After church on Sundays, they used to play in the fields, while "in the summer etc. we used to get into [Waltham] chace or forest & occa-

sionally on Saturday afternoons or holidays made parties &
walked to a place called Yew Tree bottom (from its abound-
ing with those trees), taking with us tea, sugar, bread, butter,
a boiler, tin cups etc. where we made fires under the trees,
toasted our bread & regaled ourselves with great delight,"
Marsh later recollected.[12] Facing the Gibsons' school was
another school, run by a Miss Wyatt, "amongst whom were 2
or 3 very pretty girls." He recalled "much looking & ogling
from the windows of the 2 schools & in church, where the
seats of the 2 schools were likewise together."[13]

Once a week Marsh, Hackman, and the other boys were
marched over to the girls' school for dancing lessons from a
Mr. Wright. Dressed in their finest clothes, they were ush-
ered into one end of a long room to await the entrance of the
ladies with their governess at the other end. In spite of
Wright's attempts to keep order, a great deal of "scrambling
& jostling" went on at these weekly events, as the boys struggled to place themselves opposite their favorites. "From these
two opposite groupes, Mr. Wright used to select one of each
in rotation to dance minuets together after which a couple of
country dances altogether concluded the business of the
afternoon."[14]

When James left school, his father arranged an appren-
ticeship for him with a mercer. As this was considered a
middle-class trade, the elder Hackman would have paid
around fifty pounds for the privilege. However, something
about the nature of his master's profession left James unfulfilled, and he did not stay to serve out the time of his articles.
In 1772 someone bought the nineteen-year-old James a commission in the Sixty-eighth Regiment of Foot. This was an
expensive step for a benefactor to take, so whoever provided

the money had great faith that James would make a success of it. Usually an ensigncy in an ordinary marching regiment, as opposed to one of the household regiments, cost upward of four hundred pounds, not including additional expenses, such as his scarlet cloth coat, his sash, his epaulette and sword, and "all [the] other necessaries, to appear as an Officer and a Gentleman."[15]

The Sixty-eighth failed to distinguish itself in its short history. Often understrength and with a reputation for shoddy discipline, the regiment formed in 1758 during the early part of the Seven Years' War. Staffed by a patchwork of officers, many of whom were Scots and Irishmen lacking elite society connections, the regiment was far too vulnerable to departmental economies to attract the most affluent and ambitious recruits. By the time Hackman joined, it was well into the seventh year of a tour of duty in the mosquito-ridden West Indies, and decimated by yellow fever. Because Hackman was gazetted while the regiment was abroad, his first experience of regimental life was probably in the Home Counties or London. (Many regiments on active service left at least one company at home to serve as a base for recruits.) The Sixty-eighth was a marching regiment, so it had no fixed address in England. Not until the reforms of 1782 was the regiment deliberately associated with a particular county. Like other marching regiments, it did, however, operate within a series of regular duty areas, encompassing most of England and parts of Scotland and Wales. Much of its work was essentially civil in nature, deploying against rioters and smugglers.

Hackman had much to learn in his first few months. Every new officer was expected to master the duties of regimental life, and he was to remain in regimental quarters until he succeeded. Some of the information he needed could be found in guidebooks, such as Thomas Simes's *Military Guide for Young Officers*, but inevitably most subalterns learned best on the job, schooled by the adjutant or his other brother officers. Some of Hackman's tasks were administrative; he had, for instance, to learn how to keep the company's books. His other concerns pertained to drill, guard duty, and the condition of the men's health and hygiene. He also had to live by the often contradictory codes of honor that melded the officer corps, such as the Articles of War that forbade dueling, although not to accept a challenge was tantamount to cowardice.

The Sixty-eighth limped back to England in the spring of 1773. A few months later on an overcast day, one of the army's senior officers, Lieutenant General Irwin, reviewed the regiment to judge their training and to ensure that their kit and uniforms were serviceable. Clearly, Irwin was not impressed. Although the officers were "properly armed" and "Expert at their Duty," he wrote, the noncommissioned officers were of a "bad appearance." The privates were a "Bad Corps & Low Sized." Their arms were clean but in a "very bad order"; and their clothing, being "much worn," was at best "indifferent." More positive was his assessment of the regimental musicians—the fifers and drummers—who beat out the orders, inspiring the men in battle. He also approved of the men's competence with their guns. However, he concluded that the Sixty-eighth was unfit for service and ordered nearly fifty men to be discharged.[16]

In July the regiment moved north toward Newcastle, via Chelmsford and Norwich. Hackman fell sick, and in October he was left to convalesce in the small cathedral city of Peter-borough, close to Huntingdon and thus Hinchingbrooke House.[17] It was during this period that he met and fell in love with Martha. It must have been more of a curse than a blessing when he regained his health and was forced to leave Peterborough for Newcastle. By then, the regiment had done much to remedy the ills brought to the officers' attention by Lieutenant General Irwin, and its annual inspection, on May 16, was a triumph. Although the condition of the men's arms was still "very bad" and the regimental surgeon was reported absent without leave, the inspecting officer, Major General Evelyn, declared that the men were a "good Body—attentive & steady & pretty upright." He concluded his review on a high note: "This Regiment promises to be a very good one, when [fully] Recruited."[18]

Recruiting accounted for part of Hackman's responsibili-ties. During the following year while the regiment was based in Scotland at Fort George, he and a small party of men reconnoitered the towns and villages. Typically, most recruit-ing parties comprised a subaltern, a couple of noncommis-sioned officers, and a drummer. They were authorized by "beating orders," signed by the king in London; "and all Magistrates, Justices of the Peace, Constables, and all others Our Civil Officers whom it may concern, are hereby required to be assisting unto you in providing quarters, impressing carriages, and otherwise as there shall be occasion."[19] Because of the war, new recruits were thin on the ground. Competi-tion for these were fierce; Hackman had to contend with other regiments and the navy. Consequently, the job of per-suading young men to sign up required a good deal of tact on his part, and he proved successful. During his recruitment drive, which also included scouring Ireland, the numbers in the ranks rose, and by December 1775 it was reported that the Sixty-eighth was "near full."[20] On the other hand, Hackman could not afford to be choosy. Government regulations laid down the following rules: enlistment oaths were to be witnessed in the presence of a justice of the peace; volunteers must be medically examined before a surgeon; full-grown recruits were not to be under five feet six inches tall; they must not be runaways, indentured apprentices, or militiamen; and finally, they must be Protestants. However, in practice, some Catholics did enlist, as did the lame, the stunted, and the weak. Other recruits joined the ranks straight from jail in return for a pardon.

During this busy time, Hackman managed to maintain contact with Martha and even persuaded her to grant him a number of assignations in London. "They indulged themselves in their love as privately as possible for a considerable time, unknown to his Lordship," wrote the pamphleteer Manasseh Dawes, who later became friendly with Hackman, "and convinced each other (particularly on his part) that all-powerful love was involuntary and unrestrained, whatever prudence might dictate for the sake of appearances."[21] According to the same source, Sandwich did find out about the relationship. Tipped off about the affair by his Polynesian guest, Omai, he confronted his erring mistress and she promised to reform. "But such were her affections for Mr. Hackman, that they overcame her in favour of him, with whom she had long secretly but periodically indulged, and compelled her to continue her intercourse with him more cautiously."[22]

Hackman's feelings for Martha continued no less strong.

As vanity often accompanies love, he understandably wanted to impress her. When in London, he ran up large bills at Charles Pearce & Son, a tailor and client of his future brother-in-law, the solicitor Frederick Booth. He must have appeared to advantage in the color green, for he ordered countless items in various shades, from a pea green Florentine silk waistcoat to a pair of sea green Florentine silk breeches. If his extravagance equaled the depth of his sentiments for Martha, he was a man completely lost; he returned to the shop many months later when fashions shifted and had a green waistcoat shortened.[23]

In early 1776 time was running out for Hackman. He was due to leave England for Ireland, where his regiment would be based for several years. He desperately wanted a commitment from Martha, and he determined to propose marriage. On February 27 he dined with Booth at an inn in Holborn before setting off for Huntingdon. It would be his first attempt at putting his relationship with her on a formal footing. Booth scrupulously recorded the date of the journey in an account book, noting that he had lent Hackman four pounds and four shillings when "he went to Huntingdon for the last time."[24] Considering the sum he owed his tailor, self-assurance must have buoyed his good mood for him to borrow so much money, no matter how good a friend he considered Booth.

There is no way of knowing where Hackman met Martha when he reached Huntingdon, but surely Hinchingbrooke House would have been impossible. If Sandwich had not been in residence, they would have had to contend with gossiping servants. Wherever the proposal took place, Martha rejected him.[25] Possibly, her refusal had to do with the children; they were Sandwich's, and perhaps she worried that she would lose them if she left the earl. Hackman might have considered these and other explanations, convincing himself that her unwillingness was halfhearted and that he still had a chance with her.

Dejected over Martha's rejection of his marriage plans, Hackman left for Ireland a few days later as planned.[26] A promotion to the rank of lieutenant failed to give him the solace he needed after Martha's rebuff, and during the first weeks of the following year he sold his commission to become a clergyman and returned to England. In turning to the church, he might have been seeking comfort for his wounded soul, though most likely he was thinking of Martha; if he had a more settled career, he hoped, she would reconsider their future together.

FOUR

Love and Madness

"*What a pity that so many . . . drones are admitted into the* Church, keen sportsmen, sharp shooters, & mighty-hunting Nimrods of the cloth, as it is called by way of eminence," remarked the conscientious William Jones, curate of Brox-bourne in Hertfordshire. "For the accommodation of the lat-ter class of these Reverends daily advertisements appear for the sale of the next presentations of valuable livings, rendered much more valuable, as being 'situated in fine sporting coun-tries'—'plenty of game'—'a pack of staunch fox-hounds kept in the neighbourhood.'"[1]

Jones was not alone in his complaints. Caricaturists delighted in depicting the typical country parson as toad-eating and tithe-loving. At his most extreme, the clergyman was said to be illiterate and a fool, a gourmandizer on his parishioners' wealth, self-satisfied, drunken, and bigoted. Then there were the nonresidents, vicars who never visited their parishes at all. Preferring the life of metropolitan loungers, they farmed out their glebe lands and put their responsibilities in the hands of a curate. Many even omitted Sunday services, a circumstance that shocked evangelicals. Part of the problem was that many advowsons were not church property and could therefore be bought and sold as readily as cows in a cattle market. For many young ordinands, a clerical career was less a vocation than a leap in the dark. Even at the lowest levels, the discrepancies in clerical incomes were huge. Most of England's ten thousand vicars earned less than fifty pounds per annum. Some parishes, however, provided extremely comfortable standards of living; their incumbents grew fat on roast capons and beef, while at the highest levels of the church hierarchy—deaneries and bishoprics, for instance—incomes might reach astronomical levels.

The scope for clerical diversification was vast. Many clergymen doubled as writers. One of the most venomous satirists of the age, Charles Churchill, was a vicar, as was the sociable and art-loving Cornishman John Wolcot, the eponymous Peter Pindar. Others wrote antiquarian histories; not a few wrote for the newspapers or the stage. Several worked as medics, while some, such as the Reverend Matthew Peters, succeeded as artists. In this respect they agreed with the professional elite's distrust of the specialist: just because a man was qualified in one area didn't mean that he couldn't try his hand at something else. Life was to be enjoyed, not endured. While poverty forced some clergymen to abandon the black cloth, others willingly discarded it at the first sign of fame or the whiff of a competence.

Of course, some of the best clergymen lived unexceptional lives. They sermonized on Sundays (twice), catechized the poor, ministered to the physical as well as spiritual welfare of the sick, inspected the local school, settled their neighbors' disputes, baptized, married, and buried. Men like these provided the foot soldiers in the Anglican church's drawn-out war against Roman Catholicism and atheism, and the much greater enemies of apathy and Methodism.

It was probably such a man that Hackman studied theology under while pursuing his orders, as there is no solid evidence that he attended a university. After he left Ireland, he settled in the south of England, at Chichester, either with or near his uncle Hyde Mathis. Mathis owned freeholds in several counties, as well as property in Gosport. Indeed, one of these holdings abutted one of Hackman's own, in the parish of Alverstoke, close to his Gosport birthplace. A few suggestive details survive from his time in Chichester. While his behavior toward others gave no immediate cause for alarm, he was depressed and solitary. According to one newspaper correspondent, he exhibited "some evident proofs of a *melancholy insanity* [my italics]." Significantly, he also made no secret of the fact that he was still deeply in love with Martha—at least his neighbors thought as much. "His connection with Miss Ray was well known here, and it was supposed by them who knew him best that he was married to her, or under some engagement."[2]

The association between disappointed or unrequited love and madness is as old as love itself. Indeed, according to the Roman statesman Cicero, love actually is a madness.[3] From classical times to the Renaissance and beyond, kings, scholars, merchants, shepherds—no social category or class has been immune—have suffered under love's tyrannical and often malevolent influence. "I had rather contend with bulls, lions, bears, and giants, than with Love," wrote the clergyman Robert Burton in *The Anatomy of Melancholy* in 1621.[4] In eighteenth-century England, Bedlam and other madhouses were full of lovesick lunatics. "Nothing shakes the mind more forcibly" than disappointed love, wrote James Boswell in 1778, "as every body may be convinced, who has curiosity and firmness to visit the receptacles of insanity, and contemplate human nature in ruins."[5]

Ancient Greek and medieval Arab physicians conceived of lovesickness as a distinct mental disease, with a graphic list of symptoms. They believed that sufferers could be recognized from the hollowness of their eyes and the continuous blinking of their eyelids. Their "breathing is disturbed," wrote Avicenna in the eleventh century; they are "either joyful and smiling, or despondent and in tears, murmuring of love; . . . all the bodily parts are dried up, except the eyes which are swollen due to much crying and wakefulness." Citing a famous experiment, Avicenna asserted that the condition could be demonstrated in a patient simply by running through a list of women's names and waiting for his pulse to waver. One of his cures for the condition was marriage. He himself had seen this cure effected. "I viewed [it] as remarkable," he wrote, "and as demonstrating that our physical nature obeys our thoughts." According to Avicenna, the illness was in many ways similar to melancholia.[6]

Later scholars and poets enriched Avicenna's list of symptoms. Shakespeare wrote of Hamlet's "unbrac'd" doublet, his "stockins fouled,/Ungart'red, and down-gyved to his ankle,"

his pale skin, trembling legs, and "piteous" look.[7] Frenchman Andre Du Laurens referred to the dejected lover's
"amourous melancholie." He wrote, "You shall finde him
weeping, sobbing, sighing, and redoubling his sighes, and in
continuall restlessness, avoyding company, loving solitari-
ness, the better to feed & follow his foolish imaginations."[8]
Robert Burton devoted much of his famous book to the condition. Like almost all of his predecessors, Burton pictured
the typical sufferer from love melancholy as male. (It was not
until the end of the seventeenth century that female sufferers
supplanted them.) Drawing on a vast body of learned authorities, he painted a colorful portrait of the despondent lover's
want of appetite, his lean build, his drooping head, and the
numerous mental symptoms that made his life so miserable.

Burton believed that the prognosis for sufferers of the
disease was grim:

> For such men ordinarily, as are thoroughly possessed
> with this humor, become senseless and mad, . . . no
> better than beasts, irrational, stupid, headstrong, void
> of feare of God or men, they frequently forsweare them-
> selves, spend, steale, commit incests, rapes, adulteries,
> murders, depopulate Towns, Cities, Countries to satis-
> fie their lust. . . . Hee that runnes head-long from the
> top of a rocke, is not in so bad a case, as hee that falls
> into this gulfe of Love. For . . . saith Gordonius the
> prognostication is, they will either runne mad, or dye.
> For if this passion continue, saith *Aelian Montaltus, it*
> *makes the blood hot, thicke, and blacke, and if the inflamma-*
> *tion get into the braine, with continuall meditation and wak-*
> *ing, it so dries it up, that madnesse followes, or else they make*

away themselves.... Go to Bedlam for examples. It is so
well knowne in every village, how many have either
died for love or voluntary made away themselves, that I
need not much labor to prove it.[9]

Although eighteenth-century doctors did not write as
picturesquely about love as Burton did, they, too, cited love
as a frequent cause of madness and suicide. To Richard Mead,
only religion matched love as an instigator of mental distress,
while William Battie wrote of the "perpetual tempests of
love" that often led to suicide.[10] In 1772 the Edinburgh professor William Cullen identified "vehement love" as one of
the principal types of melancholia. Like other eighteenth-
century doctors, he distinguished the condition from satyria-
sis and nymphomania. Jerome Gaub, in his influential *De
regimine mentis* of 1763, wrote, "How often do beautiful maid-
ens and handsome youths, caught in the toils of love, grow
ghastly pale and waste away, consumed by melancholy,
green-sickness, or erotomania, when delays occur or the hope
of possession is lost?"[11]

To some eighteenth-century writers love was best
avoided altogther. James Thomson, author of the enormously
successful poem *The Seasons,* railed against love, mapping out
how predatory females ruined men's capacity for public business and politics. His sweetheart absent, the "aspiring
Youth" of book one of his poem embowers himself in "glim-
mering Shades" and "sympathetic Glooms" and howls
beneath "trembling" moonbeams.[12] In similar style, the
Oxford scholar Thomas Warton, in his 1772 poem *The Suicide,* pictured a gifted young man driven by penury and hopeless love to kill himself:

Full oft, unknowing and unknown,
He wore his endless noons alone,
Amid the autumnal wood:
Oft was he wont, in hasty fit,
Abrupt the social board to quit,
And gaze with eager glance upon the trembling flood.

If only, a "cherub voice" then opines, the youth had called upon religion's aid, he would have endured his afflictions more patiently.[13]

Yet at the same time as these writers censured victims of unrequited love, their compelling descriptions of distracted youths contributed to powerful currents that sentimentalized them. During the eighteenth century, thanks in large part to the rising status of women, all sorts of errant behaviors earned pity and respect, and tales of doomed and hopeless love found eager readerships.[14] In Henry Mackenzie's best-selling 1771 novel, *The Man of Feeling,* the hero Harley dissolves into tears on encountering a lovesick woman in Bedlam. "My Billy is no more!" she wails. "Do you weep for my Billy? Blessings on your tears! I would weep too, but my brain is dry; and it burns, it burns, it burns!" In *Tristram Shandy* and *A Sentimental Journey,* Laurence Sterne earned plaudits everywhere for his winsome portraits of the love-melancholic "poor Maria."[15] The best and most evocative true stories of ill-fated lovers, such as that of Italian swordsman Joseph Faldoni and Frenchwoman Theresa Meunier, two inconsolable souls who made a double-suicide pact and shot each other, were honored all over Europe. Their tragic love affair climaxed in front of an altar at a chapel in Lyon during the summer of 1770. Forbidden by Theresa's father to marry, they each tied a piece of pink ribbon to one of the pistols, then gave the ribbon to the other, who pulled it. Thereafter, devotees of the couple's story sought pieces of the ribbon as romantic relics, and Jean-Jacques Rousseau, the apostle of sentimentalism, composed an epitaph for them.[16]

During the eighteenth century, cases of men maddened by love included the writer Thomas Creech, who hanged himself "(As 'Tis Said) for Love," and the sordid Peter Ceppi, an Italian, who was hanged for wounding his former lover, Henrietta Knightly. Turning up at her London lodgings on the morning of Queen Charlotte's birthday, January 18, 1778, and finding the frightened woman alone in the garret, he locked the door, flourished two pistols, and said that he was *come to do {her} business*." Although Mrs. Knightly managed to escape through a hole in the lower panel of the door, she was wounded in her breast. At Ceppi's trial it was revealed that the couple had once lived together and that Mrs. Knightly had promised to marry him. Apparently, two days before the incident, Ceppi's landlady had overheard him telling Mrs. Knightly that he would shoot himself in her presence and "lay his dead bones on her side" unless she returned to him. "I told him he was a fool," Mrs. Cross pithily informed an Old Bailey jury, thus proving herself anything but a romantic, and "he should not come any more into [my] house."[17]

Perturbed by the new sensibility, doctors and clergymen voiced anxiety about the nation's physical and mental well-being. Writing as early as 1733, the eminent Dr. George Cheyne had warned his countrymen of the dangers of rich living and opulence. It seemed to him then that the state of excessive sensibility that luxuries and England's peculiar soil

and unpredictable weather had engendered had opened a
Pandora's box of illnesses, from mild amnesia and hypochon-
dria to insanity and suicide. Cheyne called his book, and thus
the condition, *The English Malady.* "The title I have chosen
for this treatise," he remarked, "is a reproach universally
thrown on this island by foreigners and all our neighbours
on the continent."[18] His remedy was a combination of light
meals, weak drink, moderate exercise, regular evacuations,
sleep, and relaxation. In short, the "Purity and Simplicity of
uncorrupted Nature."[19] Other writers called the condition
"the Spleen." Thus Oliver Goldsmith, writing in his *Citizen
of the World* essays of the 1760s: "I now found my whole system discomposed. I strove to find a resource in philosophy
and reason; . . . I saw no misery approaching nor knew any I
had to fear, yet still I was miserable."[20]

Like many contemporary writers, Cheyne was convinced
that England was the suicide capital of the world. "The *English* die by their own hands with as much indifference as by
another's," wrote Frenchman Beat Louis de Muralt in 1725.
" 'Tis common to hear People talk of Men and Women, that
make away with themselves, as they call it, and generally for
Reasons that would appear to us but as Trifles."[21] Writers
like Joseph Addison, who glamorized suicide for the stage,
added to the impression. So did the journalists who reported
zealously upon the subject. During the 1770s rarely a day
passed without at least one London newspaper recording a
suicide. "Wednesday morning a reputable tradesman in Holborn desired his wife to get up and make him a bason of tea,
being rather indisposed," reported the *General Evening Post*
for 8–10 April 1779. "When she returned, she found him
lying on the floor, with his throat cut."[22] Nine days later the

same newspaper printed another suicide story from the west end of town. Thus a "person of note" was discovered dead in his study. "He had left a note upon a table, signifying . . . that he had lost the greatest part of his fortune by gaming, and had many debts of honour, which he was not able to pay."[23]

While Dr. Cheyne had offered a mixture of climatic and sociological reasons for the nation's ill health, other writers blamed the national fondness for tea or meat, while still others cited the lack of religious restraints or the Englishman's peculiar freedoms. "The Englishman pulls up the collar of his overcoat above his nose and steals away, each man according to his own humour, one prophesying, one being converted, and another shooting himself," wrote one German writer in 1775. "Fortunate is he who, under so lowering a sky, has a good conscience and is not in love, or who at least does not love in vain; or he will cut his throat like Lord Clive, shoot himself as my neighbour did of late, or hang himself, as a pretty young creature of sixteen years of age did last Saturday."[24]

For many, killing oneself for love added a noble quality to death, and no one emblematized this mood better than the German writer Goethe. Intensely sensitive and a melancholic himself, he spoke for a whole generation of world-weary youths, to whom life without romantic illusions was quite simply unbearable. His epistolary novel, *The Sorrows of Werter* (1774), took the reading world by storm, sweeping up the young and impressionable in its path and outraging moralists everywhere. A simple yet affecting tale, it focuses on Werter's passion for a young woman named Charlotte. Unable to marry her (she is betrothed to the dull but honorable Albert), he shoots himself in the head with one of Albert's pistols. The book is full of Werter's commentaries on life. He is arrogant and artistic, highly wrought and intelligent. Quick to praise the so-called "natural" responses of people less sophisticated than himself (in particular, peasants and children), he has nothing but contempt for the straitened behavior of his adult male contemporaries. Apparently, the novel inspired a rash of Werter-like suicides all over Europe. In England, in November 1784, the *Gentleman's Magazine* blamed Goethe for the death of a young woman at Southgate named Miss Glover. "The *Sorrows of Werter* were found under her pillow," it noted disapprovingly.[25]

Possibly Hackman's notoriety sparked the first English publication of *Werter*. Just two weeks or so after the murder of Martha Ray, the newspapers carried advertisements for the so-called Daniel Malthus translation, which was published by Dodsley in Pall Mall. Almost at once, readers and critics noticed the similarities between Hackman's plight and Werter's own, and on April 30 a letter was published in the *Public Advertiser* reinforcing the parallel. "Sir," it began, "I have just read a Book called The *Sorrows of* WERTER, a German Story, founded on Fact; and could not help being struck with the very remarkable Resemblance, in some of the Circumstances, between WERTER'S Story and that of the unfortunate Mr. *Hackman*. If any one should entertain a Doubt that Love was capable of working upon the Passions of Mr. *Hackman* to such a Degree of Violence as to make him commit the desperate Act . . . let him read WERTER, whose Story is very well written by the English editor, and he will, I think, no longer doubt of it."[26]

Indeed, Werter's shattering, epistolary legacy to the

woman he loves is a masterpiece of Romantic self-absorption, and could have been recited by Hackman himself: "It is all over.—Charlotte, I am resolved to die; I tell it you deliberately and cooly, without any romantic passion. The morning of that day on which I am to see you for the last time; at the very moment when you read these lines, Oh! best of women! a cold grave holds the inanimate remains of that agitated unhappy man, who in the last moments of his life knew no pleasure so great as that of conversing with you. . . . I will die.—It is not despair, it is conviction that I have filled up the measure of my sufferings."[27]

Significantly, a tradition evolved to the effect that Hackman had himself been carrying a copy of Goethe's book on the night that he murdered Martha Ray. Thus not once but twice was his reputation caught up with that of Werter. The story was erroneous, but it is easy to see how it arose, for according to another highly successful book, Herbert Croft's epistolary novel about Hackman and Martha Ray (for which, see appendix 5), Hackman was one of Goethe's most enthusiastic readers.

In February 1779 *Hackman was ordained as a deacon* and priest; then, on March 1, the bishop of Norwich instituted him to the living of Wiveton in Norfolk. This remote and windy parish near the East Anglian coast was then in the gift of his uncle Hyde Mathis, so it may have been intended for him for some time. It wasn't worth much, but it was something, "under £50," according to a contemporary document, though Hackman was convinced that he could make more from it.[28]

A priest now, with all that the title implied in terms of respectability and success, he renewed his pursuit of Martha Ray, convinced in his own mind that she had actually agreed to marry him. At one point he arranged a meeting with her friend Caterina Galli and persuaded the singer to ask Martha if she had forgotten their discussion of late February or early March 1776. (Galli's presumption in talking to Hackman offended Martha, and for some weeks Martha refused to dine with her.)[29] On or about March 30 he wrote a desperate letter to Martha. He would carry this letter to Covent Garden on the fatal night. Like his letter to Frederick Booth, it, too, included talk of suicide.

My dearest Life!

I never think of you but with a pleasing pain, the consequence of that love of which, I hope, I have given you every proof in my power. I never bring you to my recollection (which I almost continually do) but with inexpressible anxiety; yet, while I know you are not wholly mine, so great is my misery, that I cannot express it; which, added to the difficulty in which, at best, we have accomplished our meetings at Marybone, and other places, and the obstacle of Lord S—between us, almost distracts me. You know my sufferings on your account are far from trifling! When therefore will you relieve them, and make that time happy, which you only have hitherto rendered irksome and anxious to me? Having quitted the army by your advice, I am now wedded to the church, have lately been presented to a living in Norfolk, and require nothing now to complete my happiness, but to be wedded to you. In

your own dear words, let us now be one. I know you
have children, and I love them, because you are their
mother. As the youngest is your particular favourite,
and indulged by maternal fondness, I shall rejoice to
have it with me when we are married. I know you are
not fond of the follies and vanities of the town. How
tranquil and agreeably, and with what uninterrupted
felicity, unlike any thing we have yet enjoyed, shall we
then wear our time away together on my living, and
my estate at Gosport! we shall have near 200l. a year
from the one, and 100l. a year from the other, which
will be enough for us in a country life. And by all the
vows you have made me, and by that stolen bliss we
have known, I do now assure you, that dear as you are
to me, and although parent of several children by Lord
S——, if you are faithless enough to forsake me, and not
embrace my offer, you'll feel for the despair it may
occasion, when, perhaps it will not be in my power to
repeat that offer to you. O! thou dearer to me than life,
because that life is thine! Think of me and pity me. I
have long been devoted to you; and your's, as I am, I
have either to die or soon to be your's in marriage. For
God's sake let me hear from you; and, as you love me,
keep me no longer in suspense, since nothing can
relieve me but death or you.——Adieu!

Your most humble,
and affectionate servant.[30]

Distressed, Martha sent the letter to the Gallis, enclosing
a short one of her own in which she asked Hackman to aban-

don his pursuit of her. This letter, which the Gallis invited
Hackman to read at their lodgings at No. 3 James Street, off
the Haymarket, on the night of April 6, was the last missive
that he would ever receive from his former mistress, and he
begged the Gallis to permit him to take it away with him.
They refused, perhaps not wishing to give Hackman evidence
of a relationship with Martha.[31]

Hackman was devastated. As he wrote to his brother-in-
law, Frederick Booth, "By some means or other," he had
"lost" her.[32] He had no idea what had gone wrong. Having
convinced himself that she had remained in love with him
during the previous three years, he now had to face the possibility that his wedding fantasy would remain just that, a fantasy. Surely, he thought, there was more to her dismissal than
a simple change of heart. Galli then added to his misery by
volunteering that Martha was tired of him and had found
someone else.[33] Galli's comment seems to have pushed him
further over the edge, for he sent a short, anonymous letter to
Sandwich, claiming that two of Martha's friends were trying
to involve her in an intrigue. "If you have any regard for Miss
R," he wrote, "you must loose [*sic*] no time in endeavouring
to break off her dangerous acquaintance with Mrs. H. t. n &
her daughter, otherwise you will loose her." Perhaps he
focused on these particular friends out of suspicion; if they
had counseled Martha against seeing Hackman early on, he
would forever view them as a threat. At any rate, Hackman
ended by warning Sandwich to be on his guard, adding that
the letter came "from one whom you have served and could
not see you injured without information."[34] The only way in
which Sandwich had certainly served him was with his hospi-

tality at Hinchingbrooke House, but Hackman hoped to give the impression of sincerity so that the earl would act in earnest.

After the murder, a friend of Sandwich's visited Hackman at the bridewell at Tothill-Fields and mentioned that Martha was innocent of any love affairs. Hackman expressed his relief, and with the realization that Galli had lied to him, he laid the fault of the murder at her feet.[35] Perhaps he had been thinking of Galli when one of Sir John's men had carried him to the bridewell after the killing, having exclaimed to his captor, *"What a change has a few hours made in me — had her friends done as I wished them to do, this would never have happened."*[36] He had certainly made one last plea to the Gallis to intercede on his behalf. On the morning of the murder, he had sent for Mr. Galli, making another request to look at Martha's letter. This Mr. Galli had refused; in any case, the letter was no longer in his possession, he had told the despairing man; therefore the matter was out of his power.[37] The question will always remain: what request was so significant that it would have prevented the tragedy from occurring? Unfortunately, the solution remained with Hackman.

FIVE

Sensation

To say that most Londoners discovered a voyeuristic delight in the Hackman murder case would doubtless be an exaggeration and unfair to Londoners. Yet it is impossible to avoid the conclusion that many people thought that something quite remarkable and fascinating had happened. If the huge quantity of newsprint was not evidence enough, there is the excited testimony of diarists and letter writers. Everyone, it seemed, wanted authentic information about the ill-fated couple.

A positively sadistic character marked much of the interest. "I have been dining with a party at Harry Hoare's," wrote Hackman's fellow cleric the Reverend Dr. John Warner, to his friend George Selwyn on April 8. "All the talk was about Miss Ray and her murderer, but no clear account yet of the latter . . . I called to-day, in coming from Coutts's at the Shakespeare Tavern, in order to see the corpse of Miss Ray, and to send you some account of it; but I had no interest with her keepers, and could not get admittance for money."[1]

To the splendidly burnished pen of Horace Walpole, gentleman and connoisseur, the murder provided yet another glorious opportunity for wit and callosity. No man was better skilled at teasing out the slightest hint of human suffering; no man more reveled in the minutiae of personal and social disaster. "How could poor Miss Wray have offended a divine?" he playfully asked one of his regular correspondents, the countess of Upper Ossory. "She was no enemy to the church militant or naval, to the Church of England or the church of Paphos.—I do not doubt but it will be found that the assassin was a dissenter, and instigated by the Americans to give such a blow to the state. My servants have heard that the murderer was the victim's husband—methinks his jealousy was very long-suffering!"[2]

Horace Walpole. Engraving, c. 1790, by B. Reading after a portrait by Sir Joshua Reynolds. He was a prolific letter writer and lively conversationalist.

On the following day he dashed off a plumper account of the case to her, partly based on private information from his friend Lord Hertford and partly from a rapid perusal of the newspapers. "Now upon the whole, Madam, is not the story full as strange as ever it was? Miss Wray has six children, the eldest son is fifteen, and she was at least three times as much. To bear a hopeless passion for five years, and then murder one's mistress—I don't understand it." It was, he added, "very impertinent" of Hackman to "rival Herod, and shoot Mariamne—and *that* Mariamne a kept mistress!"[3]

To another correspondent, the Reverend William Cole, Walpole wrote in a more philosophical vein; he was now convinced that Hackman was mad, "and the misfortune is, that the law does not know how to define the shades of madness." He added ironically, "You dear Sir, have chosen a wiser path to happiness by depending on yourself for amusement. Books and past ages draw one into no scrapes; and perhaps it is best not to know much of men till they are dead."[4]

Lady Ossory raised the frightening possibility that the unseasonably hot weather had affected men's brains, thus provoking an outbreak of stalking and violence. She instanced a number of cases, including one involving a former lieutenant in the East India Company's service, one James Craggs, who was besotted with a Miss Maria Clavering, as well as another involving one of Sir Joshua Reynolds's nieces. "He [the stalker] came a few days since to Sir Joshua's; asked if she was at home; and, on being answered in the negative, he desired the footman to tell her to take care, for he was determined to ravish her (pardon the word), whenever he met her." The delightful frisson she experienced in relating this anecdote wasn't lessened when she thought of her young friend "Mie Mie," the attractive daughter of the Marchesa Fagnani and the reprobate fourth duke of Queensbury, who was then on holiday in Paris. "Keep our little friend at Paris whilst this mania lasts," she conjured, "for no age will be spared to be in fashion, and I am sure Mie Mie is quite as much in danger as the person I quoted in my first page."[5]

She didn't doubt that Craggs was mad, she added. But what could be done? Apparently he was keeping a watch on Miss Clavering's uncle's house; and "scenes" were "daily expected even in the drawing-room." Yet another man she mentioned had actually "sworn" to shoot a "Miss Something, *n'importe*," if she did not run away with him from the Opera house.[6] One titled lady of her acquaintance refused to leave her house for fear that she would be murdered.

Newspapers fed the public's appetite for "authentic" details about Martha and Hackman with biographical information and anecdotes from anonymous "correspondents." There were no honors to be won in this department of journalism, and their authors mixed fact with speculation. "Mr. Hackman, now the topic of conversation, is descended from a very reputable family," wrote one of them in the *General Evening Post*. "It is said that the murderer of Miss Ray will be executed on the spot where the deed was done, as has generally been ordered in such extraordinary cases," wrote another in the *Gazetteer, and New Daily Advertiser*.[7] One very likely contributor of newspaper paragraphs, in the days immediately following Martha's murder, was a young lawyer named Manasseh Dawes. Later Dawes befriended Hackman and wrote a pamphlet about the affair: *The Case and Memoirs of the Late Rev. Mr. James Hackman*. Soon it was public knowledge that Hackman had once been an army officer, and that he had first met Miss Ray at Hinchingbrooke House. "After that he saw her several times, both in town and country, [and] in one of his visits, it is said, he proposed marriage to her, which she declined, and, to prevent any disagreeable consequences, never after admitted him to her presence," wrote a correspondent in the *Morning Chronicle*. "This, it is supposed, induced him to commit the horrid act."[8]

Typical in detail and tone was the same paper's account of the murder:

The following are the most authentic particulars that we can collect of the unhappy murder which was perpetrated in the Piazza of Covent-garden theatre on Wednesday night:—Miss Reay, the unfortunate victim, was coming out of the play-house, accompanied by two friends, a gentleman and a lady, between whom she walked, when she was met by the man who committed the fact. He stepped up to her without the smallest previous menace, or address, put a pistol to her head, and shot her almost instantly dead. He then fired another at himself, which, however, did not prove equally effectual. The ball grazed the upper part of his head, but did not penetrate sufficiently to produce any fatal effect; he fell, however, and so firmly was he bent upon his own destruction that he was found beating his head with the utmost violence with the butt end of the pistol, by Mr. Mahon, apothecary, of Russel-street. He was carried to the Shakespeare Tavern, where his wound was dressed. In his pockets were found two letters; one a copy of what he had written to Miss Reay, and the other to his brother-in-law, Mr. Booth, of Craven-street. The first of these epistles is replete with warm expressions of affection to the unfortunate object of his love, and an earnest recommendation of his passion. The other contains a pathetic relation of the melancholy resolution he had taken, and a confession of the cause that produced it. He said, he could not live without her person, which he had so long admired, and since he found by repeated application, that he was shut out from every hope of possessing her, he had conceived this design as the only refuge from a misery which he could not support. He heartily wished his brother-in-law that felicity which fate denied him, and requested that the few debts he owed might be discharged from the disposal of his effects. When he had so far recovered his faculties as to be capable of speech, he enquired of Mr. Bond, with great anxiety concerning Miss Reay: being told she was dead, he desired that her poor remains might not be exposed to the observation of the curious multitude. About three o'clock in the morning Sir John Fielding was sent for from Brompton, who came to town about five, and not finding the assassin's wounds to be of so dangerous a nature, ordered him to be conveyed by Mr. Bond to Tothill-fields Bridewell, where he now lies in a fair way of recovery, and under the guard of a person set over him, to prevent any future attempts upon his life. The name of this ill-fated criminal is Hackman; he is a clergyman at present, but about four years ago was an officer in the army: not meeting with success in the military profession, by the advice of his friends he soon after quitted it, and assumed the gown.[9]

Few writers in the newspapers or magazines shed any tears for Martha. At best, they portrayed her as charitable and as a benevolent mistress to her servants. Most described her as "hapless" or "unfortunate." A.Z., writing in the *Westminster*

Magazine at the end of April, even adopted a flippant tone about her death:

> *Without one kind enlight'ning* Ray,
> *She's gone to everlasting day;*
> *Or else (O may I not be right)*
> *To everlasting realms of night.*[10]

Almost all of the public's sympathy went to Hackman. After all, he was not a common murderer; he had killed Martha Ray under the influence of a romantic obsession. In the words of a poet, writing in the *Gazetteer, and New Daily Advertiser*: " 'Twas *love*, not *malice*, gave the direful wound."[11] It also counted in his favor that following the murder he was docile to a fault and that he was a clergyman. "Don't you pity that poor devil Ld Sandwich just now, & the poor girl too, & and I think the poor man too; tho' I think it quite right he should be hanged, I pity him monstrously," wrote Charles James Fox's aunt Lady Sarah Lennox to her sister Lady Susan O'Brien.[12] Yet the charity shown Hackman failed to move everyone, most notably the feminist "Sabrina," who wrote a series of letters to the *Morning Chronicle* on the subject. She attacked those who wept for Hackman as "Barbarians," stating that she would "drop the tear of real sensibility" on Martha's grave.[13]

The most damning criticism of Hackman came by way of comparison; adverting to an earlier and, in some respects, similar murder, one writer accused him of putting "human nature to the blush." "The unhappy Mr. Naughton, who shot Miss Knox in Ireland [during November 1761], was far less blameable than the murderer of Miss Reay; the former never intended to kill the Lady he loved to distraction; it was against her father he bent his rage, because that Gentleman opposed Mr. Naughton's union with his daughter; it was against him he levelled his pistol, and Miss Knox's filial piety urging her at that instant to throw herself between her father and the pistol, the shot went off, and she saved a father's life at the expence of her own, who to restore the unfortunate murderer would willingly have forfeited, if possible, many lives."[14]

Although it was not unusual for clergymen to face criminal charges, cases involving the possibility of execution were extremely rare. Capital punishment was designed to degrade its victims, and one of the purposes of establishment law was to ensure that Anglican clergy were not publicly humiliated. The best-known exception was the almost contemporary case of the Reverend Dr. Dodd, a popular and talented London preacher, executed in April 1777 for forging a bond in the name of one of his former pupils, Philip Stanhope, fifth earl of Chesterfield. The case was something of a cause célèbre at the time, provoking a huge public outcry. Curiously, it also preempted the Hackman case in some of its details.

Dodd, who was born in 1729, first rose to fame during the 1760s as a flowery sermonizer and zealous supporter of a number of distinguished London charities. Cultured and highly ambitious, he was a chaplain-in-ordinary to George III by the age of thirty-five, counting many influential aristocrats among his friends and patrons. He was a copious writer: sermons, poems, and magazine articles flowed from his pen; he even published a roman à clef and put together a popular Shakespeare anthology. He was attractive in manner, well dressed, and handsome. Often he could be found at Ranelagh and Vauxhall Gardens; he loved gossip. In other words, he enjoyed life.

His connection with his nemesis, Stanhope, began in 1765, after the boy's godfather, the famous fourth earl of Chesterfield, witnessed one of his sermons. Impressed, the earl appointed Dodd his godson's tutor, charging him with overseeing the boy's religious education and social development. Dodd was, the earl told the boy's father, "the best and most eloquent preacher in England, and perhaps the most learned clergyman" he had ever known.[15]

The arrangement lasted until 1771, after which time the tutor and his charge saw little of each other. Stanhope embarked on the Grand Tour of Europe while Dodd continued his career in London. Unfortunately, Dodd soon found himself involved in a number of scandals, not least of which was when his wife was caught trying to bribe her husband's way into a vacancy in the fashionable parish of St. George's, Hanover Square. Consequently, the king struck him off his list of chaplains.

By the winter of 1776, he owed large sums of money to several local tradesmen. He was unable to pay his rent, and his furniture was about to fall into the hands of creditors. It was then that he embarked on the scheme that was to bring about his ruin. On February 1, 1777, acting as he said on the new earl's behalf (Stanhope had succeeded Chesterfield as fifth earl in 1773), he approached a stockbroker named Lewis Robertson with a spurious story. Handing Robertson a bond, Dodd explained that the earl was deeply in debt and had instructed Dodd to raise forty-two hundred pounds on the document. The earl had not approached Robertson himself, he explained, because discretion was of the utmost importance and the earl

THE REV.^D DR DODD.

London. Pub.^d May 24. 1777. by J. Walker N.º 13. Parliament Street.

The Reverend Dr. Dodd. Engraving, 1777, by an unknown artist. A handsome likeness of a man known for his vanity.

did not want to arouse the suspicion of his servants. He had therefore delegated the task to Dodd, trusting to their friendship and his financial acumen. Robertson was somewhat in awe of Dodd, and knowing nothing of his troubles, the stockbroker agreed to see what he could do, at the same time promising to act with equal discretion. Robertson then began a concerted search of London's banking houses, alighting at last on a certain Fletcher, a partner in Raymond and Company, who agreed to lend the money but only under strict conditions. These Dodd agreed to, and on the following morning he returned to Robertson with the bond duly signed with what purported to be the earl's signature.

However, a problem arose over the legibility of part of the document, and on February 5 Fletcher's solicitor approached the earl and part of the scheme quickly unraveled. The peer denied all knowledge of the bond, and Dodd and Robertson, who was initially thought to be party to the forgery, were placed under arrest. Dodd returned the money, but it was not enough to secure his freedom and on February 8 he was taken to the Guildhall and charged with forgery.

There he presented a pitiful sight. Barely able to raise his voice above a whisper, he called upon the earl to remember their friendship, protested his innocence in heartrending tones, and finally, at the end of his speech, collapsed into a flood of tears in the witness box. He had had "no intention to defraud" Lord Chesterfield, he told the court; he had been "pressed extremely for three or four hundred pounds to pay some tradesmen." The money was meant merely as a "temporary" expedient; he should have paid it back in half a year. "My lord cannot have forgot, that he is under some obligations to me; he must have some tenderness towards me; he knows I love him; he knows I regard his honour as dearly as my own! I hope he will, according to the mercy that is in his heart, show clemency towards me," he added.[16] It was, most people agreed, a remarkably pathetic speech. However, he did not succeed in moving everyone, and at the end of the hearing the earl and Fletcher were bound over to prosecute.

The trial took place at the Old Bailey on February 22 and became one of the most talked-about legal events of the century. Each day brought forth some new anecdote of the "unfortunate divine": he was close to death from starvation in his cell in Wood Street Compter; he attempted to escape disguised as a butcher; his wife, Mary, was mortally ill with a "hysterical disorder"; it was even said that he attempted suicide.[17] Meanwhile, by six o'clock, hours before the doors of the Old Bailey had even been opened, would-be spectators crammed the surrounding streets. Huge sums were offered for the best seats in the court, and there was a near riot when some law students, who had been promised a special gallery to themselves, were denied access.

Dodd offered much the same defense as he had given at the Guildhall. He did not refute that he had forged Chesterfield's signature, but he did deny that he had intended to swindle his former charge. This was an important point to stress, for he was accused of forgery with an intent to defraud, which carried the death penalty. Just as Hackman would do, Dodd made a ritual invocation of death. "My lords, oppressed as I am with infamy, loaded as I am with distress, sunk under this *cruel* prosecution, your lordships, and gentlemen of the jury, cannot think life a matter of any value to me; no, my lords, I solemnly protest that death of all blessings would be the most pleasant to me after this pain!"[18] Yet, he recollected, he had a wife, an "unparalleled example of conjugal attachment and fidelity," and creditors, too, "honest men," who would lose much by his death. He therefore hoped that, if just "for the sake of justice towards *them*," some mercy would be shown him.[19]

Unfortunately for Dodd, the trial judge, Baron Prryn, was not easily impressed. During his summing up he made light of Dodd's arguments, and the jury returned with a verdict of guilty. Henceforth, Dodd was, in a sense, a dead man, and when on May 16 his sentence was passed, it was indeed death by hanging. In the meantime, however, his case had attracted a huge amount of support. People remembered his charities; he received visits from well-wishers and letters of condolence from all over the country. It did not seem fair that Dodd should suffer the same penalty as a murderer or highwayman.

According to the fencing master and writer Henry Angelo, sorrow about the case became a sort of "national epidemic."[20] Not surprisingly, Dodd's plight in Newgate evoked a series of petitions. Charities, trades, parishes, the Methodists, Oxford and Cambridge universities, private individuals, Englishmen abroad, the jury at his trial, the Corporation of London—all pleaded with the king to show mercy. One Bristol man wrote complaining that he had not been able to sleep since Dodd had been sentenced to death, while another man offered to have himself "publickly Whipt" from Charing Cross to the Bottom of Long Acre on three separate Mondays, and to undergo "one full years Imprisonment in Utter Darkness" if that could be accepted as a proper atonement.[21] The largest petition, drafted by Samuel Johnson, came from the "Gentlemen, Merchants, and

Traders, [and] inhabitants of London, Westminster, and the borough of Southwark."[22] Measuring some thirty-seven and a half yards long, it contained upward of twenty-three thousand signatures. However, neither it nor any of the other petitions proved successful, and on June 27 Dodd was driven out of Newgate, taken to Tyburn, and executed.

*Before the court could decide Hackman's fate, a dis*traught Sandwich launched his own inquiry into the circumstances of his mistress's death. After a restless and turbulent night, on the morning of April 8 he dashed off a short, desperate letter to one of his closest friends, naval captain Robert Walsingham. "For gods sake come to me immediately," he wrote, his hand palpably trembling, "in this moment I have much want of a real friend; poor Miss Ray was inhumanly murthered last night as she was stepping into her coach at the playhouse door."[23]

Apparently Walsingham calmed the man down by counseling restraint. What was the point of hating Hackman? Miss Ray was dead. Nothing would bring her back. And so he left Sandwich, remarkable as it may seem, not with hate in his heart but in a mood of Christian forgiveness.

Presumably Caterina Galli had still not recovered from the shock of her friend's death when Sandwich attempted to interview her later that day, for he was only able to speak to her husband. Having spent the night in a room at the Admiralty, she left London early that morning for her apartments at Chelsea.[24] Possibly she was really ill, in which case she had a right to keep to her bed, or maybe—and it is not difficult to find some presumptive evidence for this, too—she wanted to keep a low profile. Naturally, people were curious about her involvement. Sandwich wanted to know what she knew of Miss Ray's movements in the days leading up to her death and, just as significant, what she knew of Hackman.

Her husband's declaration in the forms in which it survives is brief and not particularly informative: "About a week ago Mr Hackman sent a letter to Miss Ray desiring he might be permitted to see her for five Minutes; in answer to which she wrote a short letter, & sent it by Mr & Mrs Galli, & sent back his own letter; Mr & Mrs Galli shewed Mr Hackman Miss Ray's letter, but would not leave it in his possession, telling him he must desist from his pursuit, for that she could have no concern with him & would not at any rate give him a meeting."[25] So, the Gallis were simply the innocent medium of a brief and unsatisfactory correspondence.

More revealing, perhaps, was Hackman's own account, which he gave to Walsingham on April 9. In his eyes, there was no doubt that he had been misled, and that the whole of the blame was Galli's. She had led him to believe that Miss Ray had taken a lover, and thus she was directly responsible for the murder. Still shackled and watched over by two of Sir John Fielding's men, he made it clear that at the time of the murder he had been out of his mind and that he had been aware neither of raising the pistol to Miss Ray's head nor, indeed, of firing it. The murder, if such it was, had been committed in a state of momentary insanity, as his intention had been to commit suicide in front of her. Later that day Walsingham wrote to Sandwich:

> Believe me it is as *much impossible* for this Poor Wretch to *escape*, as it is for him to recall what is past. Sir John

said to day the Depositions would hang a nation. . . .
He wishes not to live himself, he told me to day he
hop'd to suffer as soon as *possible* . . . Her innocence
being cleared up, & your forgiveness as a *Christian*, is
all he wishes for, but all the Powers on earth *cannot*
save him, his great fear is being anatomized, not on his
own account, but his family's.

He does not deny having kill'd her (poor creature)
but says he was not sensible of it at the time. I beg for
god's sake you'll so far make your self easy, by being
assur'd that he will suffer the law as speedily & certainly as the Fact was committ'd.[26]

Meanwhile, Sandwich decided to send Martha's body to
Elstree in Hertfordshire, so that she could be interred in the
parish church in a vault in the chancel next to where her
mother lay. During the evening, he arranged for her corpse to
be removed from the Shakespeare Tavern to an undertaker's
shop near Leicester-Fields, where it could be decently prepared for burial. With remarkably bad taste, some newspaper
correspondents preoccupied themselves with the fate of her
jewels: would they or would they not be buried with her?
One correspondent estimated their value at near two thousand pounds. Others speculated over her burial dress. Apparently, she was not wrapped in a shroud; rather, Sandwich
insisted on her being coffined in the same clothes that she
had died in.[27]

Earlier that day, at just after nine o'clock in the morning,
the governor of Tothill-Fields, George Smith, brought Hackman up to Sir John's private office in Bow Street. This second
"presentment" was in addition to the indictment found by

the coroner's court at the Shakespeare's Head Tavern, and it allowed Hackman to be formally examined. As was expected, a large crowd waited outside in the road, and when the cavalcade appeared, onlookers jostled the witnesses. Departing from his usual procedure, Sir John guided Hackman away from the public room into a private annex. All were then barred, except some few wealthy and titled spectators.[28]

Hackman was in a terrible state. His bandaged head gave him an odd, almost eccentric appearance, and according to one correspondent, "from the agonizing pangs which entirely discomposed and externally convulsed him," it was some time before Sir John could call the court to order. Many people, some in tears, shifted in their seats uncomfortably. Indeed, Hackman's "manifest agitation, contrition, and poignant grief, too sensibly affected all present to wish to add affliction to such heart-felt misery, by judicial interrogations." His voice barely audible, Hackman asked for a glass of water, which given him, helped to steady him. Sir John then "pathetically and very tenderly" requested him to compose himself and to behave "like a man" as he still had "a great deal to go through."[29] There was then a further delay when some of the witnesses signaled that they were not ready to proceed. While all of this was going on, Hackman often relapsed and then, as his attention was recalled again and again to the business at hand, he had to collect himself. A court official then called in the witnesses one by one, and as Bond, Sir John's chief clerk, read their statements, Hackman convulsed every time either Martha's name or the manner of her death was mentioned. When asked to speak, he made no attempt to palliate his offense but repeated his wish to die. This speech was again met by answering sobs from the spec-

Sir John Fielding. Engraving, c. 1775, by an unknown artist. The portraitist emphasizes Sir John's amiable character.

tators.. "Upon the whole," wrote one correspondent, "it was impossible to behold him without pity."[30]

When Sir John told him that he would be removed from Tothill-Fields to Newgate, Hackman balked. At Tothill-Fields he had a room to himself, and he was clearly alarmed at the prospect of sharing a cell with, as he put it, other "unfortunate wretches." Sir John, however, quickly put his mind at rest. He told Hackman that he might have "every indulgence" as his "former situation in life demanded," though he would have to be watched, bearing in mind his earlier attempt to commit suicide.

"God preserve you, Sir," said Sir John.

"God bless you, Sir," Hackman replied.[31]

He was then led from the house to a waiting coach and carried to Newgate. Later, on April 10, Sir John wrote a revealing letter to the earl. Having received a missive from Sandwich, presumably recommending mercy, Sir John replied, emphasizing that the case was receiving his undivided attention. He wrote:

> I am clearly of Opinion that the Evidence against
> Hackman is full and compleat to the last degree, and
> that he can make no Defence that would not aggravate
> his guilt and tend to his Conviction; but will not neg-
> lect any Hint that your Lordship gives. As to Insanity,
> it cannot be offered in excuse as it appeared and can be
> proved that he was rational and sensible of his Wicked-
> ness at 4 in the morning, when I examined him; and
> has been so ever since. To convey Comfort to you in the
> smallest degree, would make me happy, but be per-

suaded that my real friendship for you, and the partiality I had for the unfortunate Lady, will urge me to
utmost Care and Attention in this dreadful Business.[32]

Sandwich's loss also influenced events in Parliament. On
April 11 he wrote to his former friend, opposition spokesman
Lord Bristol, begging him to postpone a debate on his conduct as first lord of the Admiralty, which the opposition
expected to win. By some terrible coincidence, he was fighting for his political life, and he had neither the strength nor
the intellect to save himself. Fortunately, Bristol responded
with a magnificent gesture; he would offer up his gout as an
excuse for the debate's postponement. "I must also beg that
your Lordship will do me the justice to believe that there is
no man in this world who felt more for you on this occasion,
nor who can be more concerned than I am for any interrup-
tion to your domestic felicity," he added in a touching coda.[33]
Although the government won the debate, for weeks afterward Sandwich's position remained precarious.

Sandwich found a little comfort for Martha's loss in the
support of his family. His niece Lady Corke came to live with
him, and she took Martha's daughter, Augusta, under her
wing.[34] Several friends sent messages or letters of condolence.
"I suppose you have heard of the late accident: pray God keep
you and yours from such severe trials," he wrote his friend Sir
John Hynde Cotton.[35] All in all, April was a terrible month.
He was struggling to stay in office, and his mistress had been
taken from him.

SIX

Newgate Prison

From the moment Hackman entered Newgate, it was clear that he was going to be treated as a very special prisoner. For a start, he was confined in the same relatively salubrious apartment as that formerly occupied by Dr. Dodd and allowed every possible indulgence.[1] Having struck up some sort of friend-ship with one of Sir John's men, Thomas Carpmeal, who had watched over him at Tothill-Fields, he was given permission to keep Carpmeal in prison with him. "It is supposed, that the reason the prisoner desired Carpmeal to be with him," as opposed to one of several other possible turnkeys, noted the *General Evening Post* somewhat dauntingly, was on account of his being a man "remarkable for a gentleness of manners not often found in people of his profession."[2]

While closely watched, Hackman was free of shackles and allowed visits from friends and the inevitable sightseers. Dur-ing daylight hours, visitors could enter the prison almost at will. Not that security was relaxed; in reality it was rather strict. Few prisoners had the guile or the wherewithal to bribe their way through its gates or over its high-walled defenses, and if caught, they inevitably faced harsh retribution, while those who did escape often became national heroes.[3]

Everyone in the capital and the provinces beyond knew about Newgate. As London's chief clearinghouse for prisoners awaiting capital trial and the condemned, it was feared more than any other prison, and none had a more unsavory reputation.

"Newgate is a dismal prison," wrote Alexander Smith in his *Complete History of the Lives and Robberies of the Most Notorious Highway-Men* (1719). "A place of calamity . . . a habitation of misery, a confused chaos . . . a bottomless pit of violence, a Tower of Babel where all are speakers and no hearers. There is a mingling of the noble with ignoble, rich with the poor, wise with the ignorant, and the [innocent] with the worst malefactors. It is a grave of gentility, the banishment of courtesy, the poison of honour, the centre of infamy, the quintessence of disparagement, the confusion of wit."[4] Smith's tone may sound melodramatic, but few people could pass through Newgate's dank and horrifying walls without experiencing some sort of intoxication. Not only did one enter a world where spiritual values had been viciously overturned, but also there was a real sense in which one's physical integrity was threatened.

"I stepped into a sort of court before the [condemned] cells," wrote Boswell, of one of his visits, in 1763. "They are surely most dismal places. There are three rows of 'em, four in a row, all above each other. They have double iron windows, and within these, strong iron rails; and in these dark mansions are the unhappy criminals confined. I did not go in, but stood in the court, where were a number of strange black-guard beings with sad countenances, most of them being friends and acquaintances of those under sentence of death." He recognized a number of notorious criminals, including another prisoner with clerical connections, the robber Paul Lewis, a clergyman's son, whom he described as a "genteel, spirited young fellow." Splendidly turned out in a white coat, blue silk vest, and silver-laced hat, Lewis reminded him of the swaggering highwayman Captain Macheath, the "hero" of his favorite play, the satirical *Beggar's Opera*. "Poor fellow!" he commented later, when he came to write his celebrated journal, "I really took a great concern for him, and wished to relieve him. He walked firmly and with a good air, with his chains rattling upon him, to the chapel."[5]

By Hackman's time, the exterior walls of Newgate were huge and fashionably rusticated. Designed by the young artist and architect George Dance (whose brother, Nathaniel, like George himself, had once painted a portrait of Martha Ray), they were deliberately meant to provoke feelings of awe and horror in passersby and the occupants. By 1775, a new sessions house (the Old Bailey) had been built, and one of three new quadrangles constructed.[6] However, the condemned cells, which had so impressed Boswell, were still in existence and would long remain so.

Probably the prison's most useful visitor during the 1770s was the Bedfordshire humanitarian John Howard, a man, in Thomas Carlyle's words, "full of English accuracy, English veracity, solidity and simplicity."[7] By force of character and evangelical fervor, this somewhat dour individual did much to awaken Europe's conscience to the condition of its prisons. During August 1779, he was surprised to find that the jail was "clean, and free from offensive scents."[8] Only a very small number of the inmates were ill, and an infirmary was under construction near the condemned cells. He counted 51 debtors and 141 felons, a relatively small population by the standards of the period. Of these 141, the majority had already been convicted; the others, like Hackman, were awaiting their trial at the next Old Bailey sessions.

The diet (for those without the means to purchase their own provisions) was a penny loaf a day, though the governor, Richard Akerman, "generously" supplemented this, Howard noted. All prisons in England had a "table of fees," and Newgate's was inscribed on a painted board hung up in the felons' court. From this, he learned that Akerman was entitled to charge each prisoner three shillings as an entrance fee upon committal to the prison. The chapel, he remarked, was a "plain and neat" building. It contained a separate enclosure for the condemned, three or four pews for the other prisoners, and two galleries, one of which was reserved solely for women. "I attended there several times, and Mr. Villette [the prison "ordinary" or chaplain] read the prayers distinctly, and with propriety: the prisoners who were present, seemed attentive; but we were disturbed by the noise in the court." Howard then made one of his very practical suggestions: "Surely they who will not go to chapel, who are by far the greater number, should be locked up in their rooms during the time of divine service, and not suffered to hinder the edification of such as are better disposed."[9]

As the prison chaplain impressed Howard, he might not have known of the man's reputation for laziness, cruelty, and indifference to the prisoners' needs. Most notoriously, at Tyburn in 1778, Villette was said to have chivied the executioner to hurry up and hang a teenager—even though he had received information that the boy was innocent.[10] Like Newgate's previous chaplains, Villette was responsible for authoring many of the condemned prisoners' accounts of their lives and last hours. These widely popular, sometimes surprisingly accurate biographies were hawked around the streets after a criminal's execution.

Unusual among prison chaplains, Villette was well rewarded for his duties. In addition to the profits from his prisoners' accounts, he received thirty-five pounds basic, a house clear of land tax, two legacies, and several other perks, the whole amounting to well over two hundred pounds per annum. Akerman, too, accepted generous compensation, for in addition to his considerable salary and a Dance-designed house in the center of the prison, he also enjoyed a virtual monopoly of the "official" beer and wine supply. Almost everybody drank in Newgate, so his profit was great. A taphouse thrived there, and alcohol, which was relatively cheap, promoted conviviality in moderate consumption. It was also argued that alcohol benefited the prisoners' health, and (in 1787) that it improved prison security, for drunken prisoners preferred sleeping to rioting.[11]

Did Hackman take advantage of the taphouse? If he did, the records are silent. Almost certainly, he kept away from other prisoners, fraternizing only with the guards. "He eat a hearty breakfast of tea, and rolls yesterday, had some veal for dinner, drinks tea, and sups with the party, whose turn it is to attend him," remarked the *General Evening Post* for April 13–15, "and expresses himself particularly obliged to Mr. Akerman, for his humanity and attention in alleviating the horrors with which he is surrounded." When questioned about his attitude to his probable fate, he still maintained his resignation; "he talks of dying with pleasure," wrote the same journalist, "and declares he will make no defence whatever, but plead *guilty* to the indictment."[12] Another contributor described Hackman as calm and "perfectly composed." He appeared sorry for his crime and truly remorseful. Everything about him suggested the "repentant murtherer."[13]

At some stage, in a widely reported gesture, Hackman wrote to Lord Sandwich, explaining in great depth the "motives" that had led him to take Martha's life and asking for his forgiveness in the "most penitential manner."[14] Sandwich's response was frank and generous. As he looked upon the "horrid action" as an "act of frenzy"[15] and as coming from Providence, he would forgive it, but at the same time it had "disturbed his peace of mind for ever."[16]

Hackman's visitors included the aforementioned lawyer and miscellaneous writer, the exploitative Manasseh Dawes. Educated at Westminster and Eton, Dawes was a very convivial person, fond of theaters and pleasure gardens. Fancying himself a libertine, as a very young man he had written a pamphlet in support of the acquitted rapist Lord Baltimore, then others on Dr. Dodd and other controversial subjects.[17] Before long, Dawes befriended Hackman and persuaded him to provide material for a pamphlet about his relationship with Martha, to be entitled *The Case and Memoirs of the Late Rev. Mr. James Hackman.*[18]

In certain respects Dawes and Hackman had much in common. Both were born in Hampshire, both had fathers who had served in the navy, and both had tried their hands at the church and soldiering.[19] Dawes certainly felt a great deal of sympathy for Hackman. He threw all of the blame for the murder on

Martha herself. Her deception and treachery in refusing to marry Hackman had, he wrote, impelled the man to madness.[20]

His "character" of Hackman is a wholesale eulogy; there is neither light nor shade, nor any of the touches that would lead the reader to imagine that Hackman was anything other than a paragon. "His manners were soothing, and his heart was benevolent. . . . He was sensible, without pride; witty, without severity; easy and polite, without affectation, and with the utmost sincerity. He had a hand open as day for melting charity, and a tear for pity. . . . His life was a comment on his doctrine; it was christian and religious without enthusiasm, and altogether such as did honour to his Maker, while it reflected the utmost pleasure and satisfaction on all who knew him."[21]

Presumably Hackman's most zealous visitor was his brother-in-law, Frederick Booth, who as a solicitor was in a perfect position to help him, though as he had helped Hackman financially in his pursuit of Martha Ray, he perhaps felt remorseful and guilty. Since the murder, he had hardly put in a day's work at his office in Craven Street, and most of his time may well have been spent comforting Hackman's grieving family.[22] His wife, Mary, was said to be "inconsolable."[23] Not only had the family been publicly shamed, but also she had lost, perhaps forever, a dearly loved brother. As for Hackman's mother, she presumably remained in Gosport, looked after by friends, as there is no record of her ever coming to see her son in London.

In spite of Hackman's protestations, it was probably Booth who organized his brother-in-law's defense, to which end he recruited Thomas Davenport, an ambitious lawyer—already well known for defending the adventuress Margaret Caroline Rudd—and another lawyer named John Silvester. Silvester would later earn notoriety as a corrupt and sexually predacious London judge, though at this stage in his career his behavior seems to have been irreproachable.

Over the next few days it was counsel's job to elicit information about Hackman's mental state and his relationship with Martha in order to represent him at the Old Bailey. Where the crime of murder was concerned, the law was clear: death by hanging, which meant that they had to persuade Hackman to change his plea. If he pled not guilty, it was just possible that something might be done for him, and his life saved for his family. For a time, however, Hackman persisted in his resolve. Although he no longer accepted the entire guilt of the crime as charged, he still thought of himself as "criminal in a high degree."[24] It was therefore only after a presumably fractious internal debate that he finally allowed himself to be cajoled by his lawyers' arguments.

Publicly, he based his change of mind on two grounds. First, because in offering a guilty plea he would, in some way, be colluding in a further attempt on his life, and second, on the grounds that it was only proper from a legal point of view that the offense should be proved and "the fact established by evidence."[25] If a third reason existed, he kept it to himself, yet it is hard to believe that he was not desperately frightened of death and, as a Christian, of his probable destination.

From his lawyers' point of view, once they established the plea, their path was an obvious one. They would base their defense on the grounds that their client had been *non compos mentis* at the time the crime was committed. Unfortunately this strategy presented quite formidable risks, though under the circumstances it seems unlikely that they could have done better for him. Traditionally, English law demanded that for a guilty verdict to be proven, *mens rea,* or criminal intent, had to be established. In other words, it must be shown to the court that the accused had been fully in command of himself at the time of the crime. Thus children could not be found guilty of a crime as, lacking the ability to make reasoned choices, they could not offend of their own free will, nor, by extension, could idiots or lunatics. The law was quite specific about this. There were numerous common-law precedents, and the distinctions were restated in any number of late-seventeenth- and eighteenth-century law books. In essence, the issue was choice: for criminal responsibility to have any meaning at all, it had to be proven that the defendant could choose between good and evil.[26]

The distinctions, however, created their own problems. How was one to tell that a defendant was really mad? Idiocy could be feigned. And was not madness itself a will-o'-the-wisp, a dissembler? What, too, of certain "partial" or "temporary" states; how were those to be judged? A person could, after all, act a model of propriety in most areas of life yet totally without control in one of them. In practice, these decisions were left to the courts. The jury had to identify a defendant as an "idiot" or "mad," prompted by his conduct, the testimony of witnesses, and the judge, who would direct them. Only in very rare cases do we hear of psychiatric testimony from professional "mad doctors" before the end of the eighteenth century, and even when we do, the results were, to say the least, ambiguous.[27]

Up to 1779, the most famous case of professional psychiatric testimony was also the first: the rather unusual case of Laurence Ferrers, an earl, indicted in 1760 for the murder of his steward, Joseph Johnson. The case is worth looking at, not least because Hackman's lawyers probably had it in their minds when they discussed his defense, and because, like Hackman, Ferrers also pled some form of "momentary" or "occasional" insanity. Ferrers, by most accounts a drunken and unstable character, first came to national attention in 1757 when his wife took the rare step of petitioning the consistory court for a divorce on the grounds of cruelty. The bishop of London summoned him to answer her charges, but he refused to do so; consequently he was excommunicated. An act of Parliament then separated the couple, and receivers, including his steward, Johnson, were appointed to run his estate in order to secure an allowance for Lady Ferrers. In Horace Walpole's words, this action Ferrers "could not bear," and suspecting Johnson of being in a confederacy against him, "he determined, when he failed of opportunities of murdering his wife, to kill the steward."[28]

On January 13, 1760, Ferrers summoned Johnson to his house near Ashby-de-la-Zouch, sent his mistress and most of his servants away, and forced the unfortunate man down on his knees. Melodramatically, he shouted, "Declare what you have acted against Lord Ferrers; your time is come—you must die," before shooting him at point-blank range in the stomach.[29] Miraculously, Johnson did not die immediately—he survived for twelve hours—and after some female servants alarmed the neighborhood, a surgeon was sent for. Ferrers meantime drank himself into a paroxysmal rage. His "passions became more tumultous," and when the surgeon arrived Ferrers swore that if anyone should attempt to take Johnson out of the house, he would shoot the would-be rescuer.[30] He then pulled the steward by his wig, declared surprise that the man still lived, as he had, some days before, tested the pistol on a thick deal board, which had shattered, then threatened to shoot him again.

With the arrival of a mob, however, the balance of forces changed. Johnson was smuggled out during the night while a collier named Curtis arrested the nobleman. Ferrers was then carried to a public house at Ashby, where a coroner's court was convened and a verdict of willful murder was given. His trial before his peers in the House of Lords between April 16 and 18 was long remembered as a defining legal event, while the status of the defendant made sure the case occupied a special place in later conservative legal ideology. Thus, during the 1790s, opponents of the "rights of man" doctrines of the French revolutionaries and their English followers argued that the trial proved the equality of all men before the law, for only in England, the argument ran, could a peer be tried for murdering a commoner and suffer execution.[31]

Due to the legal customs of the day, Ferrers, by and large, conducted his own defense, which he handled badly. The facts of the case being proven, he rested his defense on a point of law, namely, that he had been of unsound mind at the time of the killing. "The defense I mean is occasional insanity of mind," he stated, "and I am convinced from recollecting within myself, that, at the time of this action, I could not know what I was about."[32] Two of his brothers attempted to substantiate his point by testifying that he, as well as an uncle and an aunt, were mad. Ferrers also called to the stand Dr. John Monro, the physician superintendent of Bedlam and one of the chief "mad doctors" of the day, but then puzzled the man with a succession of ill-considered and counterproductive questions. Determined to secure a definition of lunacy that would embrace his own case, he asked the doctor, for example, whether carrying an offensive weapon without any obvious cause could be considered a symptom of insanity. Was "spitting in the looking-glass, clenching the fist, and making mouths" a symptom of lunacy? he asked. Did walking in a room and talking to oneself and making "odd gestures" qualify?[33] Unfortunately, Monro would only answer in general terms; sometimes they were, sometimes they weren't, he stated, and he either would not or could not give a definition. In his closing speech, the solicitor general was unimpressed by Ferrers's arguments.

> If there be a total permanent want of reason, it will acquit the prisoner. If there be a total temporary want of it, when the offence was committed, it will acquit the prisoner: but if there be only a partial degree of insanity, mixed with a partial degree of reason; not a full and complete use of reason but . . . a competent use of it, sufficient to have restrained those passions, which produced the crime . . . if there be thought and design; a faculty to distinguish the nature of actions; to discern the differences between moral good and evil, then upon the fact of the offence proved, the judgment of the law must take place.[34]

The assembled peers were in no doubt that Ferrers had been of sound mind when he shot Johnson, and by a unanimous verdict they found him guilty. He was executed at Tyburn.

SEVEN

A Public Example

Just after nine o'clock on the morning of April 16, Hackman, dressed in his black clericals with his head still partially bandaged, began the short journey from his apartment in Newgate to the bar of the Old Bailey accompanied by Manasseh Dawes. Booth, who had been with him during the earlier part of the morning, remained outside, too overcome with grief to endure the additional ordeal of the arraignment. Perhaps it was for the best, for when Hackman entered the court, he was crying and shaking.[1]

Not surprisingly, the court was crowded. Besides the judge and the deputy recorder, the sheriffs and the numerous other legal officials, a whole portrait gallery of famous and distinguished faces packed the building, including the leering Middlesex MP, the notorious John Wilkes. Everyone expected high drama; most expected to shed tears; few were not prepared to be moved in some way by an unusually affecting courtroom tragedy. For every John Wilkes quipping at the sight of an attractive woman next to James Boswell, there were several more like the countess of Upper Ossory, who were genuinely moved by Hackman's predicament.[2]

The jury chosen for the occasion was the First Middlesex Jury, one of four juries of twelve men, impaneled for the three full days of the sessions. Collectively they would try more than forty cases, involving about seventy prisoners. Although the number of cases may seem excessive, it was actually routine; even complicated cases took only a few hours from the opening of the trial to the verdict. Not only was the business expedited by the rarity of jury challenges, but witness testimony was generally still fresh, while most of the defendants had already been "pretried," by either Sir John Fielding or some other magistrate, and their examinations forwarded to the court as evidence.[3] Hackman's case had taken just nine days to reach the Old Bailey.

Once the court was brought to order, the blind and aged Sir John Fielding rose from his seat and opened the proceedings by reciting the indictment. He then asked Hackman how he would plead, and a palpable hush followed. "Not guilty, sir," came the tremulous answer.

Henry Howorth, the chief prosecuting counsel, then offered a short outline of the prosecution's case, at the same time ambiguously observing that he would not aggravate Hackman's predicament by making any remarks but would leave the facts "to bear their own Construction."[4] The fact that Hackman was up against an extremely clever lawyer was not the least of his misfortunes. Howorth was highly regarded in the legal community, with a reputation for winning cases. The first witness he called was John M'Namara.

"You was coming from the playhouse with Miss Ray on the 7th of April?"

"I was. On Wednesday the 7th of April, seeing Miss Ray in some difficulties at the playhouse, and, being a little acquainted with her, I was induced to offer my assistance to hand her to her carriage; she took me by the arm."

"What time of night was this?"

"Past eleven o'clock, I believe; I am not precise to the time. As we came out of the passage that leads into Covent-Garden playhouse, when we were in the piazzas, very near the carriage, I heard the report of a pistol."

"You was not with her then; you had only handed her to the piazzas?"

"I came out of the passage with her. I had not quitted her at the time the fatal accident happened; she had hold of my hand at the time. After I came out of the passage in the piazzas I heard the report of a pistol, and felt an impression on my right arm, the arm she held with her left, and which I conceive to be the ball, after it had passed through her head, that had hit my arm."

M'Namara then added that Miss Ray had "instantly dropped" onto the pavement.

"How far had you proceeded from the playhouse door, when this accident happened?" asked Howorth.

"Within two or three yards of the front on the outside, in the street, within two steps of the coach; she had got out of the portico; it was in the piazzas that it happened. I thought the pistol had been fired out of wantonness; I had not an idea that there was a ball though I felt the impression on my arm. I stooped to assist her in a fainting fit, as I conceived it to be, through the fright of the pistol."

"Did you at any time observe the prisoner?"

"No, I did not; I do not know he was the person at all, but from what passed afterwards in the Shakspeare. I threw myself upon my knees to attempt to help her up, and found my hands bloody; I then had an idea of the truth of it, and by the assistance of a link-boy I got her into the Shakspeare tavern. Upon the prisoner being secured, I was induced to ask him what could possess him to be guilty of such a deed? or some question of that sort; and he answered me by saying, that it was not a proper place to ask that question, or something to that effect. I am not precise as to his answer."

M'Namara then described how he had asked Hackman for his name, and whether or not he knew anybody locally. "He said, he knew a Mr. Booth, in Craven-street in the Strand, and desired he might be sent for. He desired to see the lady. I did not tell him she was dead; somebody else did. I objected to his seeing her at that time. I had her removed into another room. From the great quantity of blood I had about me I got sick, and was obliged to go home."

"When the prisoner heard the lady was dead did he make any observations in your hearing?" Howorth asked.

"I cannot recollect that he made any observation."[5]

The next witness sworn was the fruit woman, Mary Anderson. Unmarried and most likely illiterate, she lived in St. Giles, a notorious slum district adjacent to Covent Garden. Presumably, she was not used to court procedures, but she seems to have enjoyed herself by giving her testimony a decided theatrical air.

"On Wednesday, the 7th of April, after the play was over, where were you standing?"

"Close by the lady's carriage."

"What are you?"

"I sell fruit."

"Give an account of all that you observed under the piazzas."

"I was standing at the post. Just as the play broke up I saw two ladies and a gentleman coming out of the playhouse; a gentleman in black followed them. Lady Sandwich's coach was called. When the carriage came up, the gentleman handed the other lady into the carriage; the lady that was shot stood behind. Before the gentleman could come back to hand her into the carriage the gentleman in black came up, laid hold of her by the gown, and pulled out of his pocket two pistols; he shot the right hand pistol at her, and the other at himself."[6]

Miss Anderson then imitated how Miss Ray had brought her hand up to her forehead before crashing down onto the pavement. The lady bled profusely, she added, and she was reminded of a "Cock with his Throat cut."[7]

"At first I was frightened at the report of the pistol, and ran away," she continued. "He [Hackman] fired another pistol, and dropped immediately. They fell feet to feet. He beat himself violently over the head with his pistols, and desired somebody would kill him."

"Whereabouts did he beat himself?" asked Howorth.

"Just about the right temple."

"His own head?"

"Yes."

"Did you see him in Tothilfields Bridewell the next day?" he asked.

"Yes."

"Was the person you saw there the person who discharged the pistol?"

"Yes."

"Is he here?"

Miss Anderson then looked toward the dock and pointed at Hackman. "That is the gentleman," she added.

Having listened carefully to Miss Anderson's evidence, Hackman's defense team, Davenport and Silvester, then asked her a number of pointed questions about the pistols. Clearly, they wanted to establish that Hackman had not gone to Covent Garden with murder in his heart but that the shooting had indeed been a matter of "momentary frenzy."

"You say Mr. Hackman pulled two pistols out of his pocket—do you mean he pulled them both out of one pocket with one hand?" asked one of the lawyers.

"He pulled them out of different pockets with different hands, and they went off just so," replied Miss Anderson, at the same time picturesquely clapping her hands in order to illustrate the staggered report of the pistols.

"Was one taken out first, and the other afterwards?"

"No; both together."

"Was the pistol cocked?"

"I saw him cock both the pistols at the same time."

"Did you see him do any thing to the pistols?"

"I saw him let them off."

Hackman's counsel then tried a different tack. "Do you know the make of [the] pistol?"

"No."

"Did you see him do any thing to the pistol before he let it off [presumably besides cocking it]?"

"No," replied Miss Anderson; she did not.[8]

At which point, Miss Anderson stood down, and Richard Blandy, the parish constable, was sworn to give evidence.

Howorth began by asking for his recollection of the fatal night.

"Coming from Drury-Lane house, as I came by the piazzas in Covent-Garden I heard two pistols go off, and heard somebody say two people were killed."

The constable described how he had discovered the apothecary James Mahon, with Hackman in hand, and how Mahon had then asked him to take the prisoner to his house in Bow Street. He ran through the same evidence that he had already given at the inquest, describing how, with Hackman appearing faint, he had carried him to the Red Lion public house instead, where he was refused admittance.

"When you saw the gentleman what situation was he in?" asked Silvester.

"All bloody," the constable replied. "He was wounded in the head. I searched his pocket and found two letters, which I delivered, as I was desired, to Mr. Campbell, the master of the Shakespeare tavern."

Silvester then asked if he had known who the letters were addressed to, and what they contained. No, replied Blandy, to both questions.[9]

Having concluded his evidence, he was then asked to stand down and James Mahon was called. "I am an apothecary," he stated. "I live at the corner of Bow-street. Coming through the piazzas in Covent-Garden, intending to go through the passage home, I had just put my foot on the first step when I heard two pistols go off. It struck me that two gentlemen had quarrelled in the boxes, and taken that method to settle the difference."

He then told the court how he had retraced his footsteps back through the piazza, and how he had discovered Hackman lying on the ground, a pistol in his left hand, beating himself violently. "I wrenched the pistol immediately out of his hand," he went on. "He bled very much. I gave the pistol to Blandy, the constable, and desired him to take the prisoner to my house that I might dress the wound, and stop the violent effusion of blood."

He then proceeded to give some details of his conversation with Campbell, of the Shakespeare's Head Tavern, but Howorth interrupted him. "It is no matter what passed between you and Mr. Campbell, did you see any thing of the lady?"

"At first I did not."

"When did you see her?"

"In the space of two or three minutes I saw her lying at the bar, supported by a person I did not know. I perceived the wound was mortal. I said I could give her no assistance."[10]

At this point he was allowed to step down, and Dennis O'Bryan, one of the two surgeons who had examined Martha Ray's body at the Shakespeare's Head Tavern, was sworn to give evidence. O'Bryan told the court how Fielding had asked him to examine the body and how he had probed the wound and discovered it to be mortal. "I felt the vessels of sensation, and tried every other way to see if I could perceive any life," he stated, but that every attempt had proved futile.[11] He then related how he had examined the wound a second time, for the benefit of the coroner.

The prosecution rested their case, and the judge, the eminent Sir William Blackstone, asked Hackman if he would like to make a statement. Did he have anything to add to what had already been said, either in point of law or in fact? Hackman wiped the tears from his eyes and pulled a small document from his pocket. As he rose, a settled hush fell over the court. Gasping for breath and barely able to speak, he struggled to regain his composure before continuing.

I should not have troubled the court with the examination of witnesses to support the charge against me, had I not thought that the pleading guilty to the indictment gave an indication of contemning death not suitable to my present condition, and was in some measure, being accessary to a second peril of my life; and I likewise thought, that the justice of my country ought to be satisfied by suffering my offence to be proved, and the fact established by evidence.

I stand here this day the most wretched of human beings, and confess myself criminal in a high degree; yet while I acknowledge with shame and repentance, that my determination against my own life was formal and complete, I protest, with that regard to truth which becomes my situation, that the will to destroy her who was ever dearer to me than life, was never mine till a momentary phrenzy overcame me, and induced me to commit the deed I now deplore. The letter, which I meant for my brother-in-law after my decease, will have its due weight as to this point with good men.

Before this dreadful act, I trust nothing will be found in the tenor of my life which the common charity of mankind will not excuse. I have no wish to avoid the punishment which the laws of my country appoint for my crime; but being already too unhappy to feel a punishment in death, or a satisfaction in life, I submit myself with penitence and patience to the disposal and judgement of Almighty God, and to the consequences of this enquiry into my conduct and intention.[12]

Customarily, most trial speeches involving wealthy or celebrated defendants were written by some friend of the accused or, with luck, by a professional or respected literary figure, such as a successful poet or dramatist. Thus Richard Cumberland, the author of a number of sentimental comedies, had written a speech for Robert Perreau at his trial for forgery in 1775 and Samuel Johnson had written a speech for Dr. Dodd in 1777. No clue hints at the author of Hackman's speech. According to Manasseh Dawes, it was "prepared" from Hackman's "own solemn words." Possibly it was Booth working from notes provided by his brother-in-law. It may even have been Dawes himself, or one of Hackman's clerical friends, such as the lecturer and curate Moses Porter. There is, however, no doubting its effect. Almost everyone dabbed their eyes to wipe away the tears; even the cheeks of the morose and habitually irritable Judge Blackstone glistened in sympathy.[13]

Afterward, Thomas Davenport rose to defend Hackman on the prearranged point of law, namely, that he had been temporarily insane at the time of the murder. In this, he was presumably aided by Judge Blackstone's own writings on the subject, for the concept of criminal responsibility occupies several pages of his standard legal textbook, *Commentaries on the Laws of England*. There, building upon earlier definitions, Blackstone defined the lunatic, or the "furious man," as one having a "defective or vitiated understanding." He went on, "In criminal cases . . . lunatics are not chargeable for their

HONORABLE
Mᴿ JUSTICE BLACKSTONE.

Honorable Mr. Justice Blackstone. Engraving, undated, by an unknown artist after a portrait by Thomas Gainsborough. The author of the *Commentaries* in full legal regalia.

own acts, if committed when under these incapacities; no not even for treason."[14]

Unfortunately, very little of Davenport's speech survives, but presumably he spoke movingly on the age-old connection between love and madness. He could have instanced the large number of lunatics in Bedlam professedly suffering from some form of love melancholy. Or perhaps he chose a more literary path, ornamenting his speech with quotations from Shakespeare or Dryden. At one point he called William Haliburton, the other constable, to the stand and asked him to produce the letter that Hackman had written to Frederick Booth in the coffeehouse. This, it turned out, was rather double-edged, but again he wanted to prove that Hackman had not set out to commit murder. For a while confusion stopped the proceedings. Blackstone was not quite certain that the letter should be read, and it was only after Howorth had given his permission that it was put before the court.[15] Afterward, Hackman's counsel having nothing more to add, Judge Blackstone summed up the evidence for the jury.

He did this in what was generally considered a masterly style, making several points in regard to the law, to the facts of the case as they had been revealed to the court, and to the contents of Hackman's letter to his brother-in-law. As the author of one of the key reference books of the period, the voluminous *Commentaries,* Blackstone was widely recognized as an authority in several fields, and he was nothing if not learned.

"With regard to the point of law," recorded a journalist, "he said, that to constitute murder it was not necessary there should be a long form of deliberation; that the bare wilfully shooting at one man, and killing another, was wilful murder; that it was also wilful murder if a man, in attempting to shoot himself, should kill another; that the prisoner had rested his defence upon a sudden phrenzy of the mind, but . . . that it was not every fit or start of tumultuous passion that could justify the killing another; but it must be the total loss of reason, and incapability of reason in every part of life."[16]

Hackman, however, had carried two pistols, which argued a "double Design";[17] as for the fact of the murder itself, that "stood uncontroverted."[18] Regarding the letter, he was "sorry to say" that that, too, argued a "coolness" and deliberate state of mind, in no way consistent with most people's ideas of insanity. "On the whole, he left it to the jury, to consider of the fact, and not the point of law; adding, that if in discharge of their consciences they were convinced that the prisoner was totally dispossessed of his reason and understanding, they would acquit; if not, they must find him guilty."[19]

Although Blackstone's summing-up may appear one-sided today, there is no evidence to suggest that Hackman's jurors were unduly troubled. Most were perhaps only too willing to be led. After all, they were not being asked to pass judgment in a political trial but to decide the fate of one ordinary man; was he or was he not guilty of the heinous crime of murder? The sort of issues that would interest a jury today, such as the precise nature of Hackman's relationship with Martha Ray, apparently went undisclosed—at least no mention of their connection was made either in the semiofficial court report or in the accounts of the trial in the following days' newspapers. Neither, apparently, were the Gallis or any character witnesses called, two surely glaring omissions.

Minutes after Blackstone had made his speech, the foreman of the jury stepped forward and delivered their verdict: "Guilty."[20] Immediately Baron Maseres, the deputy recorder on the bench, rose and passed sentence. Hackman was to return to Newgate, from whence he was to be taken "to the Place of Execution," to be hanged by the neck until he was "dead! dead! dead!" and his lifeless body handed over to the Company of Surgeons for dissection.[21]

Hackman remained calm as he listened to this terrible sentence. As the court dissolved once more in tears, he bowed to the bench and to the jury, and then "with the most perfect composure and fortitude," he could muster, he turned his face away from the court and retired.[22] Approximately one and a half hours had passed since he had entered the dock. His fate had now been decided.

EIGHT

Boswell and Hackman

There was something uncomfortably personal about James Boswell's response to Hackman's conviction. Whereas the fate of most men caught up in London's malign system of executive justice left Boswell cold, Hackman had already inspired in him a good deal of heart searching. As an ambitious Scottish lawyer, lecherous and unfulfilled, he looked at Hackman and recognized some of his own proclivities. What else was his melancholy if not a disorder of the mind? Who was to say that his obsessive pursuit of women would not end in his destruction? His copious journals record a man driven almost to despair by lust, as year after year he recounted a series of unsavory couplings with prostitutes. A lapsed Calvinist with a disabling fear of death, yet volatile and promiscuous, Boswell did not discriminate; no woman of an inferior class was ever really safe from his advances. Although he dreamed of a sentimental attachment, he was inescapably a creature of the flesh. He enjoyed fine manners, but it was the "civil nymphs" of the Strand and Edinburgh's back streets that he really liked, especially when his ardor was fueled by the drinking binges that increasingly weakened his conscience.[1] "As I was coming home this night, I felt carnal inclinations raging through my frame [and] determined to gratify them," ran a typical entry from March 25, 1763, "I went to St. James's Park, and, like Sir John Brute, picked up a whore. . . . She who submitted to my lusty embraces was a young Shropshire girl, only seventeen, very well-looked, her name Elizabeth Parker. Poor thing, she has a sad time of it!"[2]

James Boswell Esquire.
Engraving, 1787, after a portrait by Sir Joshua Reynolds. Boswell as Scottish laird and man of letters.

Anxious and guilt-ridden, he took his sexual problems to some of the great men of the day: Jean-Jacques Rousseau; the Corsican nationalist Pasquale de Paoli; and Samuel Johnson, who advocated chastity.

"I should like to have thirty women," he told Rousseau. "If I am rich, I can take a number of girls; I get them with child; propagation is thus increased. I give them dowries, and I marry them off to good peasants who are very happy to have them. Thus they become wives at the same age as would have been the case if they had remained virgins, and I, on my side, have had the benefit of enjoying a great variety of women."

"Oh, [but] you will be landed in jealousies, betrayals, and treachery," replied the Genevan sage.

Still Boswell persisted: "But cannot I follow the Oriental usage?" And then, "I should like to follow the example of the old Patriarchs."[3]

His long-suffering wife, Margaret Boswell, whom he married in 1769, was both patient and solicitous. As long as he was honest, generally she tolerated his affairs, though she balked when he fell in love with her niece, their children's nurse, Annie Cunningham. "She was much affected and told me she had come to a resolution never again to consider herself as my *wife*, though for the sake of her children and mine, as a *friend,* she would preserve appearances," Boswell confided gloomily to his journal.[4]

A less sensitive man would perhaps have followed the advice of his friend John Wilkes and rejoiced that, to paraphrase historian Lawrence Stone, sex and literary achievement went together. But Boswell was never a philosophical libertine; he merely enjoyed sex too much to easily have enough of it. Although he did go through periods of abstinence, these were almost invariably short. "He was driven by direct, uncomplicated physical needs," writes Stone, "to him as simple and instinctive as urinating or excreting."[5]

For some ten days—in fact, since the first reports had appeared in the newspapers—the Hackman case had occupied much of Boswell's time, punctuating his conversation and even dictating his movements. As a former soldier, Hackman should not be hanged but rather should be blasted from the mouth of a cannon, he had told Edmund Burke—honorably, "like the grenadiers in the East Indies."[6] To Boswell there was nothing very extraordinary about Hack-

man's act of murder, nothing that could not be philosophi-
cally explained, and it was perfectly "natural" that a man in
Hackman's position would shoot his mistress.[7]

Having already made a number of abortive attempts to
see Booth, Boswell first ran into him outside the court.
Leaving as soon as the verdict was pronounced, he found
Booth, fists clenched, pacing up and down near Newgate.
Boswell told him the verdict, and Booth asked how his
brother-in-law had behaved. "As well, Sir, as you or any of
his friends could wish," Boswell replied. "With decency,
propriety, and in such a manner as to interest every one
present. He might have pleaded that he shot Miss Ray by
accident, but he fairly told the truth: that in a moment of
frenzy he did intend it."

"Well," said Booth, "I would rather have him found
guilty with truth and honour than escape by a mean evasion."[8]

Pleased with this interview and conscious that, having
attended the trial, he would make a popular figure in London's drawing rooms, Boswell dashed over to the offices of
the *Public Advertiser*, where he intended to write an account of
the trial for the paper's editor, Henry Woodfall. By the time
he arrived, however, Woodfall had already commissioned
someone else to do the job—a "blackguard being" was hard
at work—so he was forced to settle for a few elaborative paragraphs.[9] Not to be entirely outdone, he then returned to his
lodgings with his friend, bookseller and publisher Edward
Dilly, and put together a long summation of his views for one
of the *Advertiser*'s rivals, the *St. James's Chronicle*.

Sir: I am just come from attending the trial and con-
demnation of the unfortunate Mr. Hackman who shot

Miss Ray; and I must own that I feel an unusual depression of spirits, joined with that *pause* which so solemn a warning of the dreadful effects that the *passion of love* may produce must give all of us who have lively sensations and warm tempers. Mr. Hackman is a genteel young man, not five-and-twenty. He was several years an officer in the Army, but having had his affections engaged by Miss Ray, he quitted that profession and took orders, having hopes that she would unite herself to him by marriage. Let not any one too rashly censure him for cherishing such a scheme. I allow that he was *dignus meliore flamma,* worthy of a more deserving flame; but she who could enchant for years, in the autumn of possession too, the First Lord of the A——ty, a nobleman so experienced in women, might surely fascinate in the blossom of courtship, a young officer whose amorous enthusiasm was at its highth.

"In love," wrote Boswell, there is a "certain delusion which makes a man think that the object of it is perfect, and that even the faults which he cannot but know she has had are purifed and burnt away" in the extreme heat of his ardor. "Thus was Mr. Hackman lately situated; but whether from mere change, to which fancy is liable, or from considerations of prudence and interest, he found that Miss Ray no longer showed the same affection towards him as formerly."

As Hackman's manners were "uncommonly amiable," wrote Boswell, so his mind and heart were "pure and virtuous," for he "never once attempted to have a licentious connexion" with Martha. Indeed, argued Boswell, "it may seem strange at first," but had Hackman been less virtuous, "he would not now have been so criminal. But his passion was not to be diverted with inferior gratifications."

Boswell continued, "He loved Miss Ray with all his soul," and "nothing could make him happy but having her all his own." He endeavored to overcome the misery born of her rejection, "but it overpowered him; and the consequences were told us today by himself in a decent and pathetic speech to Mr. Justice Blackstone." He described the audience as being "affected in the tenderest manner by this speech, and by a letter from the prisoner to his brother-in-law which he intended should be delivered after he had fallen by his own hands, and in which he prayed for blessings upon his mistress and entreated his brother-in-law, if ever it should happen that she should stand in need of assistance, to give it for the sake of his departed friend."

Boswell argued that this letter proved that Hackman did not set out to kill Miss Ray, though he also thought that Blackstone was right in observing that at the moment he fired the pistol at her, the intent existed, which did, indeed, establish the crime of murder. Boswell could not help but admire Hackman's "candour and honourable regard to truth" in acknowledging that in his frenzy, he had meant to kill Miss Ray. This paragon of virtue was to be applauded for not taking the defense that when Miss Ray turned to see Hackman, the first pistol, which he had aimed at his head, had taken "*by chance* a direction towards her head." But Hackman, the soul of goodness, "disdained falsehood or evasion."

Boswell then reprinted a long extract from one of a series of articles he was writing called *The Hypochondriack* for Dilly's *London Magazine,* a "periodical paper peculiarly adapted to the people of England," and which, he hastened to add, could be bought from the booksellers monthly.

To return to the passion of love with all its feverish anxiety, that being the principal subject which I wish to keep in view in this paper, it is to be observed that there is in it no mixture of disinterested kindness for the person who is the object of it. We have indeed many poetical instances of an affectation of this, where a rejected lover prays for blessings on his Delia, and hopes she shall be happy with a more deserving swain. But we may be certain that these are false expressions, for the natural sentiment in such a situation is hatred, and that of the bitterest kind. We do not feel for her who is the object of our amorous passion anything similar to the natural affection of a mother for her child, of which so fine a test is related in the Judgement of Solomon. . . . On the contrary, the fondness for the object of our love is purely selfish, and nothing can be more natural and just than what Lucy in the *Beggar's Opera* says to her dear Captain Macheath, "I love thee so that I could sooner bear to see thee hanged than in the arms of another." The natural effect of disappointed love, however shocking it may appear, is to excite the most horrid resentment against its object, at least to make us prefer the destruction of our mistress to seeing her possessed by a rival.

To support this observation, he instanced the newly notorious case of the infatuated John M'Naughton, who had shot

Miss Knox, in Ireland. "And so strong was the sense of untutored mankind in [Knox's] behalf that the populace rose in a tumultuous manner to rescue him from justice, and the sentence of the law could not be fulfilled but by the aid of a large body of soldiers."

Boswell concluded his letter with a heartfelt appeal to his fellowmen to reflect on their own sins lest they be tempted to judge Hackman too harshly.[10]

Perhaps because Boswell's identification with Hackman was so complete, he was still in a depressed state of mind later that evening when he attended a meeting of the so-called Literary Club. Founded at the suggestion of Sir Joshua Reynolds in 1764, this was the celebrated club where controversial topics were routinely aired. Boswell was extremely proud of his membership. Not only did it bring him the company of society figures like Sheridan and the Whig leader Charles James Fox, but it also carried with it its own impress of intellectual competence: he, too, was part of literary London. That night the party was particularly select with just eight members present—Sandwich's friend Sir Joseph Banks, Reynolds, Sir Charles Bunbury, Shakespearean scholar George Steevens, Samuel Johnson, bibliophile Topham Beauclerk, Boswell, and a new member, the young peer Lord Althorp.

With Boswell present to stir things up, some ill-tempered exchanges about Hackman passed among the gentlemen. In particular, they argued about the significance of the two pistols; did they or did they not prove that Hackman had intended to commit murder? Johnson, following Blackstone, reasoned that they did. Why else would Hackman have carried two pistols when one would have been suffi-

cient? This opinion, how-
ever, was controverted by
Beauclerk, on the grounds
that Hackman had probably
considered that one of the
pistols might not have gone
off, and that therefore having
two pistols was merely a matter of prudence. He offered
Johnson two anecdotes in
support of his opinion. First,
the case of Lord Charles
Spencer's cook, who shot himself with one pistol and lived
"in great agony" for ten days,
and second, the case of a cer-

Samuel Johnson, LLD.
Engraving, 1793, by J. Parsons
after a portrait by Sir Joshua
Reynolds. Hester Thrale commissioned Reynolds's portrait of
Johnson to hang in her library
at Streatham.

tain unfortunate Mr. Delmis. Apparently, poor Delmis, "who
loved buttered muffins but durst not eat them because they
disagreed with his stomach," had eaten three muffins on the
day of his suicide, knowing that he would not have to put up
with indigestion. He, too, had had two pistols. One was
found primed on the table beside him after he had shot himself with the other.

Here, however, Johnson interjected, in his characteristi-
cally bullish fashion. "You see here one pistol was sufficient."

"Because he was dead," snapped back Beauclerk smartly.
And then, "This is what you don't know, and I know."

There the conversation seemed to have ended. As even
the hero-worshipping Boswell admitted, Johnson had spoken
out of turn. Even if one pistol was sufficient to kill Delmis, it
didn't necessarily follow that two pistols would not have

been necessary. The first pistol might have misfired, or like Lord Spencer's cook, Hackman might have been merely wounded. He might also have instanced the case of the Honorable John Damer, who shot himself dead in the Bedford Arms in Covent Garden in 1776, after losing a fortune gambling; he, too, had two pistols handy.

Some minutes later, however, Johnson returned to the subject. Conscious of Lord Althorp and Sir Charles Bunbury, "men of the world to whom he was little known," who might also think that they had a right to treat his opinions cavalierly if he let Beauclerk's comment pass, he addressed himself once more to his adversary. "Mr. Beauclerk," he said, "how come you to talk so petulantly to me as, 'This is what you don't know and I know'? One thing I know which you don't know: that you are very uncivil."

"Because," replied Beauclerk, "you began by being uncivil." And then, in a lower tone, so that Johnson wouldn't hear, "which you always are."

And there the subject was allowed to lapse again. However, later the conversation turned to Hackman's inability to control his temper and Johnson began once more. "It was his business to *command* his temper, as my friend Mr. Beauclerk should have done a little ago," he commented.

"I should learn of you," replied Beauclerk.

"You have given *me* opportunities enough of learning, when I have been in your company," Johnson replied sourly. "No man loves to be treated with contempt."

Fortunately, here Beauclerk offered the older man an olive branch. Although Johnson was rude and dictatorial, Beauclerk knew him to be anything but a vicious man, and it would be a tragedy to part enemies. "You have known me twenty years and however I may have treated others, you may be sure I could never mean to treat *you* with contempt," he told Johnson.

"Sir," said Johnson, thus bringing the conversation to what might otherwise have been an uncivilly abrupt conclusion, "you have said more than was necessary."[11]

Meanwhile, Hackman, having returned to Newgate, was moved out of his apartment and lodged in one of the prison's condemned cells, where he would remain until the fatal Monday morning. There, with presumably little more than the most basic accoutrements—a rug, rope mat, Bible, and prayer book—he prepared himself to face his final moments.

He was still allowed visitors, and a clergyman friend, the Reverend Moses Porter, offered comfort. Following the example of their founder, John Wesley, who often ministered to the condemned, several Methodists wrote to tell Hackman that they were praying for him, and an anonymous woman confided via the post that she had fallen desperately in love with him. He also received a laconic note from Sandwich: "If the murderer of Miss Ray wishes to live the man he has most injured will use all his interest to procure his life."[12]

Hackman, however, remained reconciled to death, though he did admit to fear of the anatomist's knife. How would his family feel knowing that he was being probed and hacked about by surgeons?[13] Who was to say that it would not preclude his chances of eternal life? Could a dissected body be resurrected? Among ordinary people, the consensus

seems to have been that it could not. Hence, the sometimes
desperate struggles at the foot of the gallows between friends
and relatives of the deceased and the city authorities.[14]

Blackstone, in sentencing him to be anatomized, had
abided by the so-called Murder Act of 1752, "An Act for better preventing the horrid Crime of Murder." Inspired in part
by Sir John Fielding's half-brother, the novelist and magistrate Henry Fielding, it was an attempt to answer a rise in the
murder rate by aggravating the sentence. "Whereas the horrid Crime of Murder has of late been more frequently perpetrated than formerly and particularly in and near the
Metropolis of this Kingdom, contrary to the known Humanity and natural Genius of the *British* Nation," ran the pream-
ble, it had "become necessary that some further Terror and
Mark of Infamy be added to the Punishment of Death."[15]
Additionally, the act empowered the judge to order that the
prisoner's body be hung in chains. However, this was usually
omitted.

Saturday came and went, and on Sunday Villette
preached the notorious "condemned sermon." And then the
days became hours. Porter stayed with Hackman till eight
o'clock at night. A true friend, he was probably the last of
Hackman's visitors to leave; and he departed with the promise that he would return shortly. Then, alone but for a
turnkey, Hackman began to pray.[16] He had much to occupy
his mind, for soon it would be morning.

NINE

This Good Old Custom

Potentially, eight public hangings took place in London and the adjacent county of Middlesex each year, one for each of the eight Old Bailey sessions. Sometimes the number of executions on each occasion could be counted on one finger, but more often they amounted to somewhere between two and five. Taking these variations into account, one historian has calculated that more than thirteen hundred men, women, and children were executed in London and Middlesex between 1751 and 1800—a far larger number than had been executed during the previous half century. Most were hanged for murder, highway robbery, or other property crimes, such as burglary and forgery. Most were young, unemployed, or semi-indigent males, many of them with Irish or seafaring connections.[1]

No Londoner had to travel far or make extraordinary arrangements to see an execution. On the whole, hangings were an accepted part of the fabric of eighteenth-century culture. Anxious parents even brought their children to them. The spectacle of malefactors' suffering, it was hoped, would teach them virtue and honesty.[2] At Tyburn, the classes promiscuously mixed; plasterers rubbed shoulders with poets, politicians with paviours. The frequency and attraction of executions was reflected in popular linguistic usage. To hang was to "dance the Paddington frisk," "to morris," "to ride up Holborn Hill," "to dangle in the Sheriff's picture frame." A hanging day was a "collar day," a "Sheriff's Ball," or a "hanging match." The hangman was the "nubbing cull." The gallows, the "deadly nevergreen." The rope, the "anodyne necklace."[3]

Until 1783, when the execution site shifted to outside Newgate, the majority of London's hangings were carried out at Tyburn, close to where Marble Arch now stands, on a triangular gallows—"the triple tree"—next to some cow fields. There, in 1760, a certain Mother Proctor erected an extensive number of seats, "let out to spectators at so many shillings per head, according to the quality of her guests and the consequence of the malefactor."[4] The promoters of the move to Newgate were motivated by a concern for public order and the pockets of wealthy aristocrats and speculators made rich by the residential development of Marylebone. The procession of malefactors from Newgate to Tyburn lacked solemnity, wrote one. "Numbers soon thicken into a crowd of followers, and then an indecent levity is heard; the crowd gathers as it goes and their levity yet increases, till on their approach to the fatal tree, the crowd becomes a riotous mob and the wantoness of speech breaks forth in profane jokes, swearing, and blasphemy."[5]

For every commentator who applauded the new dispensation, a conservative demurred. "The age is running mad after innovation," Samuel Johnson complained, "all the business of the world is to be done in a new way; men are to be hanged in a new way; Tyburn itself is not safe from the fury of innovation." When someone suggested that the new drop-style gallows at Newgate was surely an improvement on the scaffold at Tyburn, he objected. "No, Sir, . . . it is *not* an improvement . . . executions are intended to draw spectators. If they do not draw spectators, they don't answer their purpose. The old method was most satisfactory to all parties; the publick was gratified by a procession; the criminal was supported by it."[6] And Boswell agreed with him.

The procession to Tyburn was public ritual on a grand scale, with votaries, priesthood, and sacrifice. Some recent commentators, struck by the mocking, sometimes subversive nature of these events, have used the term "carnivalesque" to describe the hanging crowd.[7] Typically, the condemned felons began their journey at about nine o'clock in the morning, when at a signal from inside the prison their shackles were struck off, their wrists bound, and they were hustled into open carts or tumbrils, alongside their coffins and the ordinary. As Johnson's remark suggests, it was important to the city authorities that their faces could be seen; if the procession was to be truly effective, the crowd had to register the felons' suffering.[8]

At the head of the procession rode the city marshal, followed by the undersheriff, the peace officers, and a large body of constables. Then the prisoners themselves appeared, followed by yet more constables and a host of javelin men. When the procession roved into sight through felons' gate, an immense cheer went up from the assembled crowd. Then, as the great bell of St. Sepulchre's sounded and the bellman or sexton read the traditional exhortation, the crowd threw fruit into the carts and pinned bouquets of flowers to the malefactors' jackets.

"All good people pray heartily for these poor sinners, who are now going to their deaths," said the bellman. "You that are condemned to die, repent with lamentable tears. Ask mercy of the Lord for the salvation of your souls, through the merits, death and passion, of Jesus Christ, who now sits at the right-hand of God, to make intercession for as many of you as penitently return unto him." He then repeated three times, "Lord have mercy upon you! Christ have mercy upon you!"[9]

The cavalcade next traveled through Smithfield, along Holborn, into St. Giles's, and on toward the Tyburn Road (today's Oxford Street), before completing its journey some two hours later at Tyburn. "Those of the lower grade, who were most eager for these sights, early in the morning surrounded the felons' gate at Newgate, to see the malefactors brought forth," recollected Henry Angelo. "These gloried in their prowess, in keeping their stations through the crowd from thence to the place of execution." Others joined the cavalcade at various stages along the route. "Hence, the crowd accumulating, on the cavalcade reaching St. Giles's, the throng was occasionally so great as to entirely fill Oxford Street, from house to house, on both sides the way, when the pressure became tremendous, within half a mile of Tyburn."[10] There were frequent stops for last good-byes to friends and relatives, and in accordance with an ancient tradition, until 1760 malefactors were encouraged to drink as much beer and wine as they could take at the taverns. Although the law was strict in most respects, it was remarkably weak regarding alcohol, failing to insist on sobriety.

The best processions were remembered for years. When Earl Ferrers was hanged in 1760, he traveled to Tyburn dressed in his silver-brocade wedding suit, "his coachman crying all the way; guards at each side . . . with a mourning coach-and-six; a hearse; and the Horse Guards."[11] Keen to avoid the merest trappings of plebian exits, Ferrers provided the hangman with a black silk handkerchief and his own white cap. Even the scaffold was hung with black crepe at the particular request of his family.

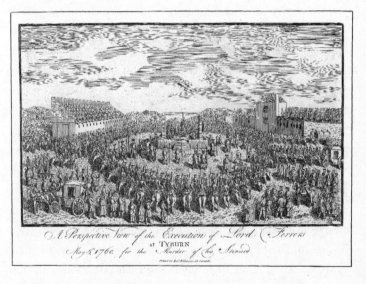

A Perspective View of the Execution of Lord Ferrers at Tyburn. Etching, c. 1790, by an unknown artist. The hangman asked Lord Ferrers to forgive him.

"Under the gallows was a new invented stage, to be struck from under him," reported Horace Walpole. "He showed no kind of fear or discomposure, only just looking at the gallows with a slight motion of dissatisfaction. He said little, kneeled for a moment to the prayer, said, 'Lord have mercy upon me, and forgive my errors,' and immediately mounted the upper stage."[12] A few minutes later the hangman pulled a lever that opened a new sort of trapdoor, which didn't work—Ferrers's toes touched the platform. So the hangman strode forward and pulled at his legs, thus effectively strangling him.

Once at Tyburn, most ordinary malefactors were taken from their tumbrils and forced to ascend a much wider cart, where they were ritualistically haltered by the waiting hangman. Above them loomed the scaffold. They then made their "Dying Speeches," and the ordinary led the prisoners and their friends and relatives in prayers and psalm singing. After about a quarter of an hour, the hangman covered the prisoners' heads in white caps and lashed the horses, which drew the carts, launching the prisoners into eternity. Some showed contrition; others rebelled. For every Paul Lewis who implored the Tyburn crowd to take warning from his fate, another prisoner went to his death cursing and protesting his innocence. Most extraordinary was the behavior of the Covent Garden basket woman, Hannah Dagoe, who attacked her executioner, ripped her clothes off, and threw them into the crowd, thereby depriving him of the bounty that his line of work entitled him to receive. She then "threw herself out of the cart, before the signal was given, with such violence that she broke her neck, and died instantly."[13]

Hanging was not a scientific procedure; prisoners were uncooperative; mistakes were made; nooses broke; beams gave way. Death came painfully, usually as the result of asphyxiation, and slowly. Often the bodies convulsed, sometimes grotesquely, discharging urine and feces. As V. A. C. Gatrell has written, "The dead body never failed to betray the nature of its experience."[14]

Stories abounded of those who escaped the gallows. Margaret Dickson "spontaneously" awoke from her coffin; William Dewell was revived in Surgeons' Hall. Best known of all was "Half-hanged Smith," who after hanging fifteen minutes was reprieved, only to return to a life of crime. When asked what his feelings were as he dangled at the end of the hangman's rope, he described a "great blaze, or glaring light, which seemed to go out at his eyes with a flash." So great was his pain on reviving, he told a contemporary, he "could have wished those hanged" who had rescued him.[15]

As the crowd encompassed "high and low," empathics and non-empathics, responses to these executions were mixed; after all, not every malefactor was a hero to the spectators. In 1767 onlookers hurled rotten fruit at the midwife Elizabeth Brownrigg, who had flogged and starved to death her apprentice. The key variables were probably group affiliation and class; "low" people favored "low" criminals, that is, people like themselves: ambitious, unlucky, and heterosexual. Almost everyone applauded upper-crust felons, hence the intense interest in Earl Ferrers and the sometimes hysterical responses to Dr. Dodd and the Perreau brothers, convicted (like Dodd) of forgery.

"I shall never forget the last execution I saw at Tyburn," Boswell wrote in 1768, "when Mr. Gibson, the attorney, for forgery, and Benjamin Payne, for an highway robbery, were executed. Poor Payne was a thin young lad of twenty, in a mean dress, and a red night-cap, with nothing to discriminate him from the many miserable beings who are penitent and half-dead with fear. But Mr. Gibson was indeed an extraordinary man. . . . He was drawn backwards, and looked as calm and easy as ever I saw a man in my life. . . . He shewed no stupid insensibility; nor did he affect to brave it out like those hardened wretches who boast that they die hard. He appeared to all the spectators a man of sense and reflexion, of a mind naturally sedate and placid."[16]

Boswell, as has been seen, was moved by suffering; he identified with a certain type of criminal. The bravery of malefactors like Gibson quieted his own apprehensions of

Mrs. Brownrigg. Engraving, 1825, by R. Cooper. Mrs. Brownrigg's notoriety earned her a place in the bestselling *Newgate Calendar.*

death. Following an execution, he felt better able to cope with life and its stresses. It taught him, he believed, that "dying publickly at Tyburn, and dying privately in one's bed are only different modes of the same thing. They are both death; they are both that wondrous, that alarming scene of quitting all that we have ever seen, heard, or known, and at once passing into a state of being totally unknown to us, and in which we cannot tell what may be our situation."[17]

Less savory was the response of a group of aristocratic and wealthy necrophiles, known collectively as "the Hanging Committee."[18] Connoisseurs of the hangman's rope, these men, publicly and without shame, immersed themselves in the paraphernalia of execution. Chief among them was the politician and wit George Selwyn, while other members included the duke of Montagu and the scholar Thomas Warton.

Everyone had a Selwyn anecdote. Sometimes on his expeditions to executions and morgues he disguised himself in a long black cloak; at other times he dressed as a woman. In 1746, when some ladies accused him of insensitivity in attending the beheading of the Jacobite Lord Lovat, he replied that he had "made amends by going to the undertaker's to see it sewn on again."[19] In 1757 he went to Paris in order to witness the attempted regicide Damien broken on the wheel and ripped apart by horses. When Charles James Fox's father, Lord Holland, lay on his deathbed, Selwyn stopped by, after which visit his lordship reportedly said, "The next time Mr. Selwyn calls, show him up:—if I am alive I shall be delighted to see him, and if I am dead he will be glad to see me."[20]

"Not only was he a constant frequenter of such scenes of horror (criminal executions), but all the details of crime, the private history of the criminal, his demeanour at his trial, in the dungeon, and on the scaffold, and the state of his feelings in the hour of death and degradation, were to Selwyn matters of the deepest and most extraordinary interest," remarked his biographer, J. H. Jesse. "Even the most frightful particulars relating to suicide and murder; the investigation of the disfigured corpse, the sight of an acquaintance lying in his shroud, seemed to have afforded him a painful and unaccountable pleasure."[21] Yet this same man was popular; his wit was admired, and he was highly esteemed by a large section of society.

It was just after five o'clock when Hackman awoke on the morning of April 19. After dressing, he prayed till quarter past seven, when a turnkey brought him a basin of tea. At half past seven Moses Porter arrived, and the friends were escorted to the chapel. Prayers were then read, and Villette gave Hackman the sacrament.[22] At this stage he seemed composed. He neither shook nor appeared in any obvious way anxious over the prospect before him. Once more, a journalist approvingly noted, Hackman admitted his guilt; his punishment, he said, was no more than he deserved; and he prayed with "all the fervency and devotion of a sincere repenting criminal."[23] He then gave Villette a note, leading to speculation that he had revealed some hidden detail about the affair, such as the exact role of Caterina Galli. Equally, however, the note could just as well have been a last letter to his family.[24]

At about nine o'clock the sheriffs arrived. They led him into the press yard, where Boswell and a crowd awaited him. Most of the onlookers had paid the prison authorities one shilling as an entrance fee. One of the sheriffs' officers slipped a rope over Hackman's shoulders, which was fastened underneath his arms with a small cord. He then began to cry. "Oh! the sight of this shocks me more than the thought of its intended operation."[25] The crowd then falling back to form a narrow lane, Porter offered him his arm, and the pair was escorted to a mourning coach, where Davenport and Villette met them.

Outside of Newgate, all was noise and bustle. According to the *General Evening Post,* the mob was London's largest since Dr. Dodd's execution.[26] Ballad sellers hawked cheaply printed broadside accounts of Martha and Hackman's relationship, each headed with an ornamental woodcut. *A Copy of Verses, on the Murder of the celebrated Miss Reay* (improbably) cast Sandwich as a hero out of medieval romance, relating how he had carried Martha to "Hinchin's tower," following her seduction by an earlier admirer. It described Hackman's wooing of Martha and her rejection of his marriage offer. In this version of events, Hackman murdered Martha in cold blood:

> A *brace of pistols he procur'd*
> *Death was his dire intent,*
> *He in the anguish of his mind,*
> *To Covent Garden went.*

Hackman received much more sympathy from the author of *The Sorrowful Lamentation and the last farewell to the world, of the Rev. James Hackman.* Writing in Hackman's own voice, the author noted that Hackman had admitted the fairness of Judge Blackstone's sentence.[27]

As the cavalcade formed with Miller, the city marshal, at its head, someone ran and told some jobbing carpenters, who

REVᴰ Mᴿ HACKMAN
Drawn from the Life. April 19. 1779

The murderer of Miss Ray the
singer

The Reverend Mr. Hackman. Engraving, 1779, by an unknown artist. Hackman, "from the Life," either at or on his way to Tyburn.

had erected a viewing platform at Covent Garden, on the mistaken notion that Hackman would be executed at the scene of his crime, that they had been bilked of their expected profit. Elsewhere in the city, in Oxford Street, the noise of the crowd frightened a dray horse, which reared and kicked a man in the head, killing him.[28]

During the journey, Hackman spoke a great deal about his family and friends, and expressed his deep regret for the great misery he had brought on them. Hatless and dressed in his customary black, he neither skulked nor attempted to hide his face; in fact, he deliberately removed his bandage so that the crowd would not be impeded in their view of him. "His whole behaviour was [now] manly, but not bold," reported a journalist; "his mind seemed to be quite calm, from a firm belief in the mercies of his Saviour."[29]

When at about ten minutes to eleven the cavalcade finally arrived at Tyburn, he walked slowly up to the black-lined cart, and with Porter and Villette on either side of him to catch him in case he fell, he climbed in. Once inside the cart, he stepped forward with "great firmness" to the front, fell on his knees, and spent fifteen minutes with Porter and Villette in prayer. Most of his thoughts were for Martha's children. He also prayed for Lord Sandwich.[30]

Hackman then turned around and walked back toward the rear of the cart, where the hangman, Edward Dennis, awaited him. Dennis, a veteran of numerous executions, was uncharacteristically polite in his behavior toward the condemned man. Perhaps slightly awed by Hackman's clerical dress, Dennis allowed Porter to help with the noose and tied Hackman's wrists behind his back with noticeable gentleness. "My friend don't be afraid of hurting me, do your duty,"

Hackman said to him.[31] Then, taking hold of Porter's hand, Hackman prayed for some minutes more before signaling to Dennis to place the white cap over him. At about quarter past eleven, he dropped his handkerchief, letting Dennis know that he was ready to die. Unfortunately, it fell into the crowd and Dennis, loathe to lose such a trophy, stooped to pick it up, thus adding an extra half minute to the wretched man's existence.[32]

Returning to the head of the cart, Dennis then whipped the horses.

Apparently, Hackman's last words were *"Dear Dear Miss Ray."*[33]

"He was no ways convulsed, nor was [there] any motion of the body that tended to shew it experienced any pain. Nothing more was to be seen than what proceeded from the jerk on quitting the cart," commented a journalist.[34] Afterward, Boswell asked Dennis if he had heard any of Hackman's conversation with the clergyman, but the executioner gave him a haughty rebuff: "I thought it a point of ill manners to listen on such occasions."[35] Someone, however, did give Boswell a description of how the rope was fixed. He then went away and drank white wine, followed by a meal of beef and porter, feeling, as he later recorded, "quite elevated."[36]

Later that day, however, he felt anxious and depressed. The dead man's image was continually in his mind, and guiltily conscious of having enjoyed Hackman's torment, he was frightened of meeting people in the streets, presumably in case he was recognized.[37] *Lloyd's Evening Post* then deepened his distress by mistakenly stating that he had traveled to Tyburn with Hackman in the mourning coach, and that he had prayed with him under the scaffold.[38] Boswell asked his friends Edmund Burke, the politician, and the tenth earl of Pembroke for advice on the subject. Burke counseled him not to make matters worse by contradicting the article. He then asked Boswell a number of rhetorical questions: "Was not you in Newgate?" "Yes." "Was not you [at] Tyburn?" "Yes." "Why then, they only sent you in a coach. Besides, why be angry at [their] making you perform one of the most amiable Christian duties: [to] visit [those] in prison?"[39]

Burke's commonsense argument only partially reassured Boswell, and he still put a disclaimer in the *Public Advertiser*. "It was not Mr. Boswell but the Rev. Dr. Porter of Clapham who so humanely attended the late unfortunate Mr. Hackman. Mr. Boswell had for a day that praise which is so justly allowed to generous tenderness; but he has taken care that it shall be enjoyed by the worthy person to whom it was due."[40]

Meanwhile, the city authorities paid Dennis two guineas for Hackman's clothes, presumably as a courtesy to Hackman's status as a clergyman, for the idea of an executioner showing off the clothes of such a victim was too unseemly to allow. The corpse was cut down after about an hour, placed in a hearse, and carried to Surgeons' Hall in the Old Bailey.[41] Having been eviscerated, on the following morning it was arranged on a wooden operating table and exposed to a large crowd who literally fought with one another to gain a good view. As they charged up the staircase, several people were knocked brutally to one side, and one journalist observed that "caps, cardinals, gowns, wigs, hats, &c. were destroyed, without regard to age, sex, or distinction.

"In the afternoon the crowd was less, in consequence of which several persons of no mean appearance thought it a good opportunity to satisfy their curiosity; but when they got upon the stair-case leading to the theatre (which was darkness invisible) they found themselves *genteelly* complimented with a shower of urine (supposed to be prepared on the occasion) issued from an instrument conducted by some persons under the stair-case."[42]

One of these visitors was the Reverend Dr. John Warner, who sent Selwyn an account of the corpse. "I saw him yesterday," he reported, "a genteel, well-made young fellow of four and twenty. There has been a deal of butchery in the case."[43]

Another visitor was Angelo, who remarked that the sight of Hackman's corpse cured him of his love of pork chops; at least, he never did eat any again.[44]

A few days later, the law and public curiosity having done their worst, Booth collected the mangled corpse, having the sad duty of organizing his brother-in-law's burial. Hackman had hoped to be buried at Elstree next to Miss Ray, but instead he was interred in the burial ground of Booth's own parish church, St. Martin-in-the-Fields, the same church where barely six weeks before the solicitor and Mary Hackman had married.[45]

The day chosen for the burial was April 24, a Saturday. In many senses, it was a grim day. Although the talk in the taverns and coffeehouses was of an accommodation with the American rebels, the latest news was bleak. The British army had won Georgia, but at a cost. The Carolinas had been exposed, and the generals were crying out for reinforcements. At about the same time as the clergyman intoned the service and the pallbearers lowered the coffin into the ground, a heavy shower of rain and hail swept down over London, darkening the white stone facing of Gibbs's magnificent steeple.[46]

And the wind carried away the voices of the mourners.

EPILOGUE

The supporting figures who had played their parts in the story of James Hackman and Martha Ray did not all long survive the protagonists. Their ordinary lives resumed, but most had their own trials to face. For some it was an early death, for others, obscurity and poverty.

The bright portents that had distinguished Frederick Booth's early career continued after his brother-in-law's death, and he died in 1831 a proud man, confident of the benefits of hard work and regularity. At some point Booth went into partnership with another solicitor, William Haslewood, and in the early nineteenth century they acted for Lord Nelson over the breakup of his marriage to Frances Nelson and the purchase of an estate at Merton in Surrey. Mary Booth died in 1807. Her husband filled the vacuum she left behind with religious observance. When Booth retired from his vestry duties at St. Martin-in-the-Fields in 1829, he must have been missed; few parishioners had worked with such selfless devotion.[1]

Sandwich lived until 1792. His lunatic wife survived him. He remained active in politics until the eve of the French Revolution in 1789, when his fortunes mirrored the fate of other of Lord North's senior ministers caught up in the debacle of the American war: dismissal, then gradual oblivion. His following dispersed and, unable to bargain for a foothold in the youthful William Pitt's administration of December 1783, he was prevented from exerting his customary influence; he never again held high office. Some preoccupations remained constant, however. The old rake did not reform, though age and worry dulled his enthusiasms. In 1787 one of the friends of the libidinous Prince of Wales wrote to him, offering a young woman as a candidate for his private theatricals. "She has played publicly six Times, but not by her own name. She is hardly twenty, stage mad, a pretty voice, and has always lived with her parents."[2] Sandwich did not accept her, but music remained his greatest love. In 1784 he devoted himself to the Westminster Abbey centenary commemoration of Handel's birth, acting as organizer, "moving spirit," and patron.[3] It was "the triumph of Handel, the commemoration, and of the musical art," recollected the oboist William Parkes. "Perhaps no band of mortal musicians ever exhibited a more imposing appearance to the eye or afforded more ecstatic and affecting sounds to the ear than this [did]."[4] The financial problems that had plagued his relationship with Martha Ray continued into old age. He borrowed liberally from a wide variety of friends and became thoroughly miserable as a consequence. In 1788 his hand began to shake as he made yet another appeal for cash, while in 1790 he was more distressed for ready money than he had ever been. He died at age seventy-three on April 30, 1792, leaving his son, Lord Hinchingbrooke, the title.

Galli never conquered the public's suspicion that she was partly responsible for Martha Ray's death. Her silence upon the subject carried the appearance of guilt. It did not help her case that she was a Catholic and a foreigner. Sensing her vulnerability, Dawes attempted to blackmail her into collaborating with him on a pamphlet describing in detail her dealings with Hackman, but she refused to help him.[5] Unable to support herself by singing and abandoned by her friends, she sank into fecklessness and poverty. Although Sandwich occasionally helped her with small sums of money, no one believed that she had not aided Hackman. An appeal to the public for money failed, and she was forced to rely on the charity of friends and a yearly benefaction from the Royal Society of Musicians. On March 3, 1797, she sang "He Was Despised" in a performance of *The Messiah* at Covent Garden, but she was not a success. "In the name of decency and common humanity, why exhibit a poor emaciated worn out old woman," remarked a writer for the *Monthly Mirror*. "We are sorry to hear Handel's divine compositions so barbarously murdered."[6] On the same occasion, the gentleman amateur Richard Mount-Edgecumb, who struck up a sort of friendship with her, described her voice as "cracked and trembling." He added, "but it was easy to see her school was good; and it was pleasing to observe the kindness with which she was received, and listened to; and to mark the animation and delight with which she seemed to hear again the music in which she had formerly been a distinguished performer."[7] Her appearance coarsened considerably toward the end of her life, to the extent that she became "rather large" and masculine-looking.[8] Surviving her husband by five years, she died in her apartments at Chelsea on December 23, 1804, aged eighty-one, and was buried in Chelsea Old Church.

Boswell forwent neither illicit sex nor executions. It has been estimated that by the end of his life, he had contracted "Signor Gonorrhoea"[9] perhaps seventeen times. It was a miserable record and he suffered mightily for it. During July 1785 the *Public Advertiser* noted that he had recently attended an execution of five convicts at Newgate. *"That* was nothing extraordinary, but it was surprising when he was followed by Sir Joshua Reynolds.—'Evil communications corrupt good manners,'" the paper added, quoting the first book of Corinthians.[10] His great public achievement, of course, was his life of his hero Samuel Johnson, a monumental work of inestimable power and fascination. No subsequent biographer has ever matched Boswell's liveliness or anecdotal cleverness. Boswell's character is on almost every page, by turns obsequious, questing, vain, melancholic, brilliant, melodramatic, and maddening. He died (most probably) of uremia in the early hours of May 19, 1795. According to his friend Edmund Malone, the Shakespearean scholar, his end was hastened by drink. He was fifty-four. "He seemed to think himself entitled to more than usual indulgence, in which he went on so rapidly that I had no longer, as formerly, any kind of influence over him."[11] Greatly missed by his many distinguished friends, he was interred on his family estate at Auchinleck in Scotland.

As for the men involved with the case, Sir John Fielding died at Brompton in September 1780. Much revered by a grateful posterity, he left behind him a reputation for fair dealing and generosity. The obituary writers praised him as one "whose abilities as a magistrate could only be equalled by his humanity as a man."[12] Because of his kindness and numerous charities, even the poor were said to regret his loss.

Henry Howorth, the prosecuting counsel, died in May 1783, at about thirty-six years of age. A keen yachtsman, he was thrown into the Thames by a sudden squall as he was boating within sight of his house at Mortlake. "Chip, never fear, we shall do very well!" he is said to have cried to his close relation Mr. Chippendale, as the two men struggled to support themselves. Unfortunately at that same moment, he was struck by the boat's mast "and was not found until about three quarters of an hour afterwards."[13] An MP as well as a leading barrister, he left behind him a grieving mistress and at least six illegitimate children. Buried in the Temple Church, he was "universally beloved," according to the *Gentleman's Magazine,* "and is greatly regretted by all who had the honour of his acquaintance."[14]

Defense attorney John Silvester, or "Black Jack," as he later became known, died in April 1822, following a night of roistering with the reprobate duke of York, the eldest brother of the former Prince of Wales. Described in 1800 as "vulgar and ineloquent," he became notorious for suppressing evidence and demanding sexual favors.[15] Such scandals, however, did not interfere with his career. Appointed common sergeant in 1790, he spent the last nineteen years of his life as recorder. His bust, which can be seen in London's Mansion House, seems to confirm the worst contemporary estimates of his character. As one of his obituaries read, he was "a man of no talent, but that of time-serving. . . . His manners like his person, were awkward and repulsing."[16]

The judge, Sir William Blackstone, died on St. Valentine's Day 1780, aged fifty-six, short of breath and corpulent. In his last years he had become ill with "water on the chest" and dropsy.[17] Law students continued to study his *Commentaries* long after his death, and they can still be read today with profit and occasional amusement. He is a remarkable stylist. Charles James Fox called him "the very best among our modern writers, always easy and intelligible; far more correct than Hume, and less studied and made up than Robertson."[18]

Hackman's executioner, Edward Dennis, died in November 1786 at his apartments in the Old Bailey, apparently "regretted in death as he was respected through life," having been well rewarded by a grateful city authority.[19] Although he had been sentenced to death for his involvement in the anti-Catholic Gordon riots of 1780, the city sheriffs had decided that he was too valuable an employee to suffer his victims' fate, so he was formally acquitted and resumed his profession. "In his office of Finisher of the Law, Surveyor of the New Drop and Apparitor of the Necklace, alias Yeoman of the Halter etc. he acquitted himself with the approbation of all but the parties concerned. He had frequently a numerous company at his levee, though all complained of a want of variety in his dish, which was hearty-choak and caper sauce," wrote a contemporary biographer.[20] Buried in the graveyard of St. Giles's on November 26, he was attended by a large crowd.

Such were the fates of the supporting actors in the Hackman murder case.

A Poem on the Death of Martha Ray

Like other eighteenth-century causes célèbres, Hackman's murder of Martha Ray inspired several poems. *The Distracted Lover. A Poem* and *Reflections on the Death of Miss Ray* appeared in book form (and were reviewed), but most of the others appeared in newspapers. *The Gazetteer, and New Daily Advertiser* published the following poem on April 17, 1779. The author was "Arcadius."

VERSES *occasioned by the* DEATH
of the unfortunate Miss RAY.

Imo in corde pudor; mistoque insania luctu,
Et furiis agitatus amor, et conscia virtus.

VIRG.

On life's uncertain road what dangers wait
  The young, the old, the fearful, and the brave!
How oft gay scenes lead on to dismal fate!
  What thousand portals open to the grave!

Ah! Hapless Ray! whate'er thy morning sun
    Had promis'd, or beheld in youth's first bloom,
Ere little more than half his course is run,
    He sees cut off by an untimely doom.

And yet no dark assassin here was found
    To wreak *his* rage—Thou fell'st not by a foe:
'Twas *love*, not *malice*, gave the direful wound:
    Not *hate*, but strong *affection*, struck the blow.

At the dire deed, when 'tis too late to mourn,
    With sad remorse recoils the murd'rer's heart;
He seeks to follow to th'uncertain bourne;
    Such mad despair can jealous rage impart!

Behold yon corse!—Ah! see the pallid hue
    Spread o'er that cheek!—Is that, that clay-cold hand
The same that Nobles press'd?—Here do we view
    Those nameless charms that could the heart command?

Ah! what avails thee, that life's brightest beam
    Play'd on thy view!—Thy S——H's sorrows shed
For thee and HINCHINBROOK alike may stream:
    His tears *embalm*, but cannot wake the dead.

Vain these are found, but *not* that lesson vain.
    How frail, alas! the tenure of our breath,
When fate thus mingles with the sportive train,
    And Love itself inflicts the stroke of Death!

Hear it, ye gay! You who in life rejoice,
    With eyes yet bright, unsully'd by a tear;
Attend Reflection—think you hear her voice
    From RAY, extended on her timeless bier.

Two Broadside Ballads

These two broadside ballads, one "popular" the other "literary," appeared in the days following Hackman's conviction.

THE SORROWFUL LAMENTATION *and the last farewell to the world, of the* REV. JAMES HACKMAN, *who is to be* EXECUTED *on April,* 19th 1779 *for the cruel* MURDER OF MISS RAY.

> Good Christian folks a warning take,
>   By me see my down fall,
> Next Monday is the fatal day,
>   My life must pay for all,
> James Hackman is indeed my name,
>   A Minister was I,
> For murder now am triy'd and cast,
>   And for the same must die.

My education finish'd at
   The University,
And first did a Commission bare,
   But no promotion see,
Four years ago assum'd the gownd,
   Alas! unhappy day.
Twas when I saw and smote was with,
   The beauty of Miss Wray.

In love I was so deep inthral'd,
   And to my lust a slave,
But as she would not give consent,
   Resolv'd her life to have,
Indeed I kill her on the spot,
   As she came from the play,
I own my sentence to be just,
   Good people for me pray.

As sure as I did murder her,
   I thought myself to kill,
But tho' I full intended it,
   I could not have my will,
No, no, from Newgate I must go,
   Unto the fatal tree
And then to Surgeon's Hall, convey'd,
   Anatomize to be.

Sad tidings to the world indeed,
   Quite shocking for to hear,
Three Ministers for to be hang'd,
   Within the space of two year,
But I a Minister worst of all,
   For to strike murder's blow,
How can I mercy e'er expect,
   That would no mercy shew.

But some things I remember still,
    And must believe them true,
That God above that reigns on high,
    Drops mercy like the due,
Likewise I've read the blood of one,
    Does cleanse us for all sin,
In him alone let me be found,
    And mercy find in him.

A Copy of Verses, on the Murder of the celebrated Miss Reay

Ye fair that grace Britania's Isle,
    Give ear unto my tale,
With due attention list a-while,
    To move it cannot fail;
A lovely girl name'd Catharine Reay,
    Adorn'd with ev'ry grace,
No tongue can tell, or pen display
    The charms of mind and face.

But she alas! in early youth
    Became the prey of man,
The base deceiver scorned truth
    To ruin was his plan;
When he'd her virgin bloom enjoy'd
    He left her quite forlorn,
Her reputation was destroy'd,
    Expos'd to public scorn.

A noble Peer beheld the dame
    Struck with her matchless charms,
He rescu'd her from want and shame,
    And took her to his arms;
For many years they happy liv'd,

Tho' not in wedlock join'd,
Of her he lov'd[,] to be depriv'd,
   What pangs must rack his mind.

Accursed be that fatal hour
   When first base Hackman came
To Hinchin's tower where he beheld
   This fair unhappy dame;
With tears he oft besought the fair
   To listen to his suit,
But she reply'd 'tis all in vain,
   I pry'thee sir, be mute.

My Lord I never will forsake,
   Who loves me as his Life,
To him I'll always constant prove,
   Tho' not his wedded wife;
Nine lovely babes to him I've borne,
   I'd not forsake his bed,
Nor leave my Infants dear forlorn,
   A monarch for to wed.

This answer soon reduced the youth,
   To absolute despair,
Like one distracted he behav'd,
   He rav'd, he tore his hair.
The sword he left, assum'd the gown,
   In hopes to ease his smart,
But all in vain the sacred garb,
   No solace could impart.

At length he cried thou cruel fair,
   Since thou refused'st to join,
With me in holy wedlock bands,
   Death soon shall make us one.

A brace of pistols he procur'd,
  Death was his dire intent,
He in the anguish of his mind,
  To Covent Garden went.

He close conceal'd in ambush lay,
  Discharg'd the fatal lead,
True to his aim the bullet flew,
  And shot her through the head.
Stung with remorse he now laments,
  That e'er he did this deed,
The hardest heart would surely melt,
  When once these lines they read.

An Essay Inspired by James Hackman's Journey from Newgate to Tyburn.

In the *Morning Chronicle* for April 23, 1779, there appears a tear-stained essay on Hackman by M*******, which epitomizes the sexual double standard of the period. Later the paper identified the author as Courtney Melmoth, otherwise Samuel Jackson Pratt, the popular writer and socialite.

THOUGHTS *written while Mr.* HACKMAN *was going from Newgate to Tyburn.*

The coaches are passing my windows in their way to Tyburn: They are crouded both within and without by people who make the morning of fate an *holiday,* and rejoice to attend the hapless culprit to the last *precipice of eternity*. The eager press of the multitude, and the throngs which appear savagely anxious to hurry on, that they may see the *most* of the misery depresses my spirits in such a manner, that, in order to my relief, I resolve to employ myself in *silent sympathy*; and instead of rushing to the scene of action, consider the *nature of the fact* that led the wretched gentleman to his suffering there. But I am stopped in the very commencement of my reflections, by the increased tumult in the streets, which are filled by the children of *cruelty* and *curiosity*; and I can almost as easily reconcile the murder itself to the laws of love and honour, as that impetuous principle which, at this instant, urges so many thousand *human* creatures to attend the execution of the murderer. Both sexes too seem to be jealously precipitate. The *female* nature is touched, and an incredible number of women are running over the pavement. In many a countenance I can, from my window, distinguish a smile, and not a few are even riotously resolved to gain the tree before the criminal is prepared to be suspended from it. The execrable shriek of one of those wretches who turn every publick or private calamity to advantage, is already piercing my ear and my *heart* with the dying words of a poor creature, not yet half way to the end of the sad journey of life. A boy, who had a solicitude to see the unfortunate pass by, is just returned, and brings me word that the culprit sat in a corner of his carriage unfettered and unalarmed. There are tears standing in the lad's eyes, and his lip is so *properly* pale, that I think highly of his heart, and reward him with a shilling, to encourage his good feelings. The greater part of London is, it appears, moving in procession along Oxford-road while I write. Alas! poor object of their entertainment, I have *no eyes* hard enough to *behold* thy passage, but have *two* to shed for thee those tributary drops of regret, and pity, that truly thou may'st claim. I forgot for a moment the cause, in contemplating the consequence, and pray to the power who alone can keep thee, that the pang which releases thee from this life shall by no means have vigour to reach the next.

But the mob is past, and I have a quieter moment to consider the circumstance that collected it together. The assigned cause of this dreadful event is *tenderness in the extreme*, and I know there have been many similar actions attributed to the same principles; but I do not, nor shall I ever, be able to believe that the *extremity* of love is *assassination of its object.* When this passion is turned into its *opposite* passion, I can conceive that the violence of the *aversion* may raise the arm against the person that inspired it. Rage, jealousy, or indignation, may all take arms, and even *kill* their object. Insanity may seize on its victim;—but I am so clearly convinced that *tender love* is incompatible with *any* idea that can *harm* its object, much less *destroy* it, that I should rather suppose this unhappy man *hated* Miss Reay, or had some *secret reason* to be *jealous* of her, or was actually under the influence of a *mental distemper,* than suppose that, merely because he could not possess her as a wife, he should put an end to her existence. And this is a strong reason why I give credit to that part of his defence which assures us his design was only against his *own* life, and to finish this in *her presence.* A desperate man who had been long brooding over his despair, and suffered his desires of *personal possession* to melt away his *delicacy,* might certainly work himself up to this—might banish reason, and summon in her absence the demon of suicide. Perhaps, too, the sick heart might dress up a kind of figure like that of *comfort* in the image of a fate so circumstanced, yet nothing but the emotions of those passions I have already described, or the utter deprivation of reason, could *connect two murders* so *peculiar.* I attribute the alteration, or rather *multiplication* of his crime, either to some glance of *scorn,* or to the *immediate ferment* of his *disorder* got to its crisis, or to the suggestions of distempered fancy, which magnified the gentleman who was with the lady into a rival or to the great quantity of brandy which, it seems, he drank at the bar of the tavern, which might add *drunkenness* to *delirium,* or else all these together in dreadful operation.

This, in the present case, is the more likely, as no former passages in the life of the offender seem to have marked that *horrid kind of vehemence* of which his last action was an example. He was of a *gentle nature*, and it is not *natural* for such to murder a *beloved* object. Their sensibility takes a different path, and almost every instance in the history of man will shew, that they oftener pine away in unoffending *melancholy*, and if ever the weapon is drawn, its point is almost invariably levelled at their own bosoms—hardly *ever* at that which produces the despair. The essays and effusions of various kinds which this extraordinary event will produce are all in prospect before me. I prophecy the teeming press, and anticipate all the sentiments of men who catch at the subjects of the passing hour. Amongst these productions I forsee the labour that will be used to prove the crime a consequence of *excessive tenderness*, and widely diffused will be the warnings, that this fact may be had in remembrance as an example to deter others against any fond indulgence of the tender ties by whose force humanity, and all its splendours are sustained.

Ten to one but that, in this waste of moral maxims, those admonitions are forgotten which are most necessary to be inculcated. Ten to one but the best inference to be drawn from the fate of poor Mr Hackman passes the public observation: yet one circumstance there is attending it, which deserves to be engraven on the tablet of every heart: There was an extreme INDELICACY in Mr. H——'s passion, which could pass over the idea of the lady's have been under a *very long personal attachment* to her *protector*. The very attempt to *wean* her from whom, even by *marriage,* argued an extravagance of something not consistent with that sweet sensation which is the *essence* of *unviolated* affection. She evidently did not give this gentleman the *preference*; for had it been so, *preference,* would have taken care (in a case where niceties *had* been dispensed with) to gratify its more lawful object. Surely this was a second deviation of that *internal* sense of *elegant* passion which asks for undivided tenderness, and for *all the heart*. To select our objects then—to consult that chaste mon-

itor that will never mislead us—to graft virtuous sentiment
on virtuous sensation—to cherish the finer touches of our
bosom as much as they will bear, without straining the con-
necting cord too hard, to admit nothing that may contradict
the principle which the dictates of *religion,* and the *customs of
a country* prescribe—and—what more? Nothing. This is all
that need be practised, and this is the moral to be gleaned
from the awful catastrophe of this morning, from *whatever
circumstances it was brought about.*

But the street is again crouded by the multitude, on
their return. Their movements are more solemn and more
slow. They walk as if surfeited with the sight they were so
solicitous to behold. The affecting ceremony is over then, as
far as it belongs to *us* to be spectators. Life *for* life is forfeited,
and the retaliating law *is obeyed.* Let us thank God that the
human debt is discharged—that the soul hath parted from a
body which can no longer feel anguish at that part of the sentence which remains; it is into our *hearts,* and our *imaginations* only, that the dismembering instruments can cut,—and
may the sympathetic terrors which we feel, and the tender
tears which our humanity drops over this *mangled corpse,* have
no *harder* effect upon us, than to restrain us from actions of
equal horror, and regulate the *best of passions* upon the *best of
principles.* I can write no more.

April, 19.   M*******

APPENDIX
FOUR

Letters by "Sabrina" and "Cato"

The public's sympathy for Hackman inspired "Sabrina" to spark the following exchange of letters in the *Morning Chronicle*. The letters appeared on May 7, 20, and 24, and June 5, 1779. The Mr. Woodfall mentioned in the letters is William Woodfall, the *Chronicle*'s printer and editor.

To the Printer of the MORNING CHRONICLE

SIR,

It has been allowed, both by ancient and modern writers, that there is scarcely a situation in life more to be avoided than being in the way of hearing the word *pity* uttered by those incapable of feelings. When an object is set up as the general *idol* of compassion, it becomes the *humble villager* to *ask* the cause of such an object's misery, before he drops the tear—*the good citizen*, as a man of commerce, whether he has preserved the laws of society; *the religious man*, whether he has observed the first of divine laws, "and done as he would be done by?" Check the tear until you know *why* it *ought* to fall; so will it fall with *double* force, or being *suppressed,* will speak the honest fortitude of a mind, which disdains being moved by false appearances.

As *real* compassion is my motive for taking up the pen, I may possibly claim some allowance for the novelty of my opinion. *Novelty* is the word I make use of to distinguish the real dictates of the heart, in opposition to the almost universal and mistaken notion of compassion adopted in the recent instance of Mr. Hackman, while the innocent victim of his ungoverned passion lies unlamented and forgotten.

I by no means wish to *stop* the tear of sensibility; I wish only to *direct it* into its *proper* channel; unconfined *merciless* pity may be compared to the *devouring deluge* bearing down *undistinguished* all before it, while the real feeling bosom may be compared to the ark, enclosing such properties only as serve to restore things to their original state, when the *intruding waters* shall subside and vanish from the *fair face of Nature.*

An endeavour to stem the strong current of false pity, and to warn your fair readers of some dangers they may shun, are my motives, Mr. Woodfall, for addressing you, when, if you express a desire for the further investigation of truth, by publishing this first letter, I shall pursue it.

Oh, Reay! I *knew thee not*, but by the *grateful* hearts who sing thy praise; yet while false pity is blubbering over they cruel murderer, I'll drop the tear of real sensibility on thy untimely grave—Barbarians!—not to weep for *thee*, and *thee alone*—snatched from every opportunity of doing that good thy heart delighted in!—snatched from thy children when most wanting the tender mother's care!—yet even these poor innocents are neglected—not even *thought* of by these fashionable PITIFUL weepers!—they *censure* thee for a *single* frailty of human nature, while they *glory* in their com-

passion for a man who has violated *all laws,* divine and human!—yet will I not totally condemn this *shadow* of compassion, as it honours the *substance.* But think, ye heedless fair! that the man who, with every tenderness, now woos you to his arms may hereafter become your murderer!—Listen then to what I shall hereafter say— reflect in the mean time, and *shun the man of violence*—be *warned!*—so shall not *Reay have died in vain!*

SABRINA.

To the Printer of the MORNING CHRONICLE

SIR,

A Sigh escaped my bosom when I saw you approved my mode of admonition; a sigh, because I had not a *less cruel* object for your approbation. Silence, a long, profound, *tear bursting* silence, did I preserve with more than Stoic fortitude, till I considered that VIRTUE in the *grave* reaps no more reward than *buried* VICE, unless some poor *enthusiast,* at the risk of being *ridiculed* as such, should endeavour to separate it from such disgraceful union.

It surely must be *allowed,* that however *faulty* Miss Reay is *supposed* to have been, she is *virtuous* in comparison with a *murderer,* therefore entitled to ALL *the pity* the shocking transaction could inspire.

Miss Reay has been blamed for living in a *criminal state* with L——d S——, yet when her sensibility had led her (from her regard to the laws of decency) to wish a *chaster connection,* and she had selected, or had had pointed out to her an object as a worthy one, and afterwards found the temper of that object too violent for her meeker disposition; if her gratitude for the many obligations she had to L——d S——, joined to her tender friendship for him, should check her design of retirement, is the *crime so great* that she is to be *deprived of life,* to expiate it? She has been blamed for giving *encouragement* to Mr. H—— (*suppose* it granted that she did) is an end to be put to her existence for merely an *indiscretion,* and he pitied for *the worst* of all crimes, MUR-DER? she unfortunately suffered the *sun-shine* of her counte-nance to beam on this man; but had she not, like the sun, a right to *withdraw* those beams? (however *warmly,* as 'tis *insinuated,* they darted on him). Is the sun always *obliged* to *shine?*—or should a cloud perchance obscure it, ought it to be *totally extinguished?*—"*Woman, thy name is frailty,*"—and are there women who weep for *him?*—Oh, *dry* your tears for *merciless* MAN! and rather weep those errors *his passions* lead you into; which, if not punished by *him* (the author of your ruin) will for ever banish you from the sweet society of virtue and honour: Then can a *woman* abandon a woman's cause?—*blush! blush!* turn your eyes inward—the man whom you now encourage to catch your smile of approba-tion, should any future prudent recollection dictate to your better judgment a change, do you not *now,* by your *ill* placed pity, confess that you think him *pardonable* for "*a phrenzy of the moment,*"—and ask your hearts, do you think you should, because a little prudence stept to your aid when settling an *irrevocable* deed? Do you think you should deserve the cruel punishment which was her lot?—Not one of you, if you will with *true* feminine feelings make *her* case *your own.*

Say she broke her engagement—is it a greater crime in *her* to have done so than in a *man?* Have not *many men* broke their engagements, even on the point of marriage? And are there not courts of *justice* to redress the injury? You say the man was driven to madness—so is that faithful animal a dog; but there is no one who does not rejoice when he is taken and hanged, while the *only* object of pity in *this* case is the person who was bit by him: But *here* your misplaced pity falls on the mad-man, and you never think of the poor creature who dies in consequence of his madness.

Mr. H. *confessed* 'twas only a phrenzy of the moment; it was allowed by all he was not mad, therefore if he had been really injured by the lady, he might, as I hinted above, have been the instrument of *public justice,* instead of being the perpetrator of *private revenge;*—but it was his *hurt pride,* ye ill-judging ones! that murdered her. Could he be said to *love* her, when he was meditating to take her from a state of affluence to share with him a state of poverty, in some obscure corner of the world? to share with him the various calamities attendant on the poor pittance of less than three hundred pounds a year, with, perhaps, an encreasing family. Can this be called *love?* No; he might imagine (as many others did) that she had accumulated riches! but herein he was (with others) mistaken: She was too *generous,* too disinterested, to take advantage of her situation, and did good for the mere *pleasure* of doing good.

I have much more to say, Mr. Woodfall, but it shall be the subject of another letter, therefore will conclude this with remarking only, that I shall be happy if we can convert any of these *retailers* of *second hand* feelings.

SABRINA.

To the Printer of the MORNING CHRONICLE,
May 20, 1779.

SIR,
Reading in your paper of to day a letter signed Sabrina, I cannot resist the impulse I have to make a few observations on the fair writer's production, whose singularity of sentiments (though expressed in good language) affected me not a little, and I cannot, as an admirer of the fair sex, but regret, that one of the community should so far be influenced by either passion or prejudice as to stand forth pub-

licly the advocate of incontinency and insincerity, both which Miss Ray, whose advocate Sabrina is, was in an eminent degree guilty of; her living with a Nobleman is a sufficient proof of the one, and her behaviour to the unfortunate Hackman, incontestibly proves the other: I could have wished therefore that pity instead of justification had been the subject of Sabrina's pen, whereby she might have avoided the discovery of her unprejudiced mind, and the little knowledge she has of the human heart: Indeed, I cannot but imagine Sabrina totally unqualified either to write or decide upon the late unfortunate affair, as I am convinced she never yet sacrificed at the shrine of the gentle deity, otherwise she would never so positively have asserted that Mr. Hackman did not love Miss Ray, merely because he wished to take her from affluence and infamy to a state of independency and credit. Surely the fair Sabrina would not wish to be understood that riches, purchased at the expence of virtue, are preferable to an honest poverty. That these hints may rectify the sentiments of Sabrina, is the wish of your constant reader.

CATO.

To the Printer of the MORNING CHRONICLE

SIR,

On a re-perusal of your Monday's paper, I read the letter signed Cato. Whether he is a descendant of the Cato of old, I know not; but from the purport of his letter we may almost conclude that he descends in a *right* line from that advocate for *self-slaughter*. Your correspondent, I presume, meant to be jocose, when he says, that I have never *sacrificed* to the *gentle Deity;*—but be that as it may, I mean not to make *him* my *confidant*: Yet he cannot surely call Mr. Hackman's a GENTLE Deity! For it must be allowed by all, that he made *his* Deity, subscribe himself a *Devil!* But with all submission to Cato's *profound* judgment, why should not Sabrina *write,* or *decide* on the late unfortunate affair, as well as he? Has not she a *right* to her *opinion* as well as he? And also a right to *give* it? Or shall we go in the old thread-bare scheme of "women should not meddle with such matters, they should mind their spinning, &c. &c. &c."—But, Mr. Woodfall, there are so many *trifling scriblers* at the present aera, that *women!* may surely be indulged with *impunity,* now and then, to amuse themselves with the pen as well as the needle; nor should *females* be discouraged, while *you* allow their productions a place in your paper.

I should esteem it a breach of politeness to accuse Cato of standing forth the *advocate* of a *murderer,* while he wishes to excite *pity* for him; though he seems not to be aware of a breach of it in himself, when he accuses me of "publicly standing forth the advocate of incontinency and insin-cerity:"—We neither of us, I should hope, contend to excul-pate either party of their *respective* FAULTS, but to place the MOST *pitiable* object in its *proper point of light*; at least I can speak for myself; and if my letters should be read again, I believe it will appear that I *warn* my sex against inconti-nency, instead of being an *advocate* for it, and that Cato him-self must be "*influenced* by *passion,* or *prejudice,*" to exhibit such a charge against me. But even *granting* Miss Reay to have been guilty of *incontinency,* is that a crime to be put in the scale against *murder?* Shall we compassionate the *crimes* of Mr. *Hackman,* and not *her's?* Can Cato pity the *enormity* of a MURDERER'S *guilt,* and at the same time urge the *frailty* of the MURDERED as a *reason* why *she deserves* no compassion?

CATO, with his *peculiar politesse,* tells me I have "dis-covered but little knowledge of the human heart,"—with what propriety I shall not now investigate; though I may venture to say that *he* has not *displayed much* of it, whatever his *depth* of knowledge *may* be.

His *hints,* by which he wishes to rectify *my* sentiments, have not had the desired effect; the singularity of *his* sentiments is not expressed in such language as in the least to *affect me,* for till MEN shew us they prefer a state of *poverty* and *virtue* to a state of *affluence* and *infamy,* few WOMEN, I am afraid, will lead the way.

I sincerely wish the world *to be what it* ought; but I believe, before *it is so,* there must be better *advocates* for *virtue* than either *Cato,* or

SABRINA.

Herbert Croft's Love and Madness

In 1780 a brilliant young writer named Herbert Croft published a remarkable book about the Hackman affair called *Love and Madness. A Story too True. In a Series of Letters between Parties, whose Names would perhaps be mentioned, were they less known, or less lamented*, which purported to contain Hackman's and Martha Ray's correspondence. In fact, Croft made the letters up. Yet he entered into his characters' predicaments so convincingly that for a long while afterward many readers thought that the letters were genuine. Not surprisingly, the book was a huge success. Its debts to Goethe's *Sorrows of Werter* were overlooked. It was even cited in books of philosophy and psychology. For Croft, it led to an introduction to Samuel Johnson and an invitation to write the life of Edward Young, the poet of the *Night Thoughts,* for the great man's *Lives of the Poets.* Yet Croft was unable to capitalize on these and other early successful publications, and by the time of his death in 1816 he was probably best known for a work that he left unfinished—an "improved" edition of Johnson's celebrated *Dictionary*.

The following extracts are from pages 1–14, 35–49, 73–75, 102–10, 117–25, and 262–63 of the first edition of Croft's *Love and Madness*. The most important of the omissions that I have made is a long letter on the boy poet and forger Thomas Chatterton, which Croft attributes to Hackman. In July 1778 Croft visited Bristol in order to interview Chatterton's family. Like Chatterton, he was fascinated by the question of personal identity, and he was determined to prove that Chatterton had forged his so-called fifteenth-century "Rowley" poems. Although Croft's Chatterton material undoubtedly confers enormous additional value upon his book, it does not add appreciably to his presentation of Hackman or Martha. Readers who want to find out more about Croft's interest in Chatterton should begin by reading the Brian Goldberg article cited in my bibliography and then turn to Chatterton's biographers.

Huntingdon, Dec. 4, 1775.

To Miss—

Ten thousand thanks for your billet by my corporal Trim yesterday. The fellow seemed quite happy to have been the bearer of it, because he saw it made *me* happy. He will be as good a soldier to Cupid as to Mars, I dare say. And Mars and Cupid are not now to begin their acquaintance, you know. Whichever he serve, you may command him of course, without a compliment; for Venus, I need not tell *you,* is the mother of Cupid, and mistress of Mars.

At present the drum is beating up under my window for volunteers to Bacchus—In plain English, the drum tells me dinner is ready; for a drum gives us bloody-minded heroes an appetite for eating, as well as for fighting; nay, we get up by the beat of it, and it every night sends, or ought to send, us to bed and to sleep. To-night it will be late before I get to one or the other, I fancy—indeed, the thoughts of you would prevent the latter. But the next disgrace to refusing a challenge, is refusing a toast. The merit of a jolly fellow and of a sponge is much about the same. For my part, no glass of any liquor tastes as it should to me, but when I kiss my M. on the rim.

Adieu—Whatever hard service I may have after dinner, no quantity of wine shall make me let drop or forget my appointment with you to-morrow. We certainly were not seen yesterday, for reasons I will give you.

Though you should persist in never being mine,
Ever, ever

your's.

Huntingdon, Dec. 6th, 1777

To the Same
My dearest M.

No—I will not take advantage of the sweet, reluctant, amorous confession which your candour gave me yesterday. If to make me happy be to make my M. otherwise; then, happiness, I'll none of thee.

And yet I *could* argue. Suppose he *has* bred you up— Suppose you *do* owe your numerous accomplishments, under genius, to him—are you therefore his property? Is it as if a horse that he has bred up should refuse to carry him? Suppose you therefore *are* his property—Will the fidelity of so many years weigh nothing in the scale of gratitude?

Years—why, can obligations (suppose they had *not* been repaid an hundred fold) do away the unnatural disparity of years? Can they bid five and fifty stand still (the least that you could ask), and wait for five and twenty? Many women have the same obligations (if indeed there be many of the *same* accomplishments) to their fathers. They have the additional obligation to them (if, indeed, it be an obligation) of existence. The disparity of years is sometimes even less.—But, must they therefore take their fathers to their bosoms? Must the jessamine fling its tender arms around the dying elm?

To my little fortunes you are no stranger. Will you share them with me? And you shall tell his Lordship that gratitude taught you to pay every duty to him, till love taught you there were other duties which you owed to H.

Gracious heaven, that you *would* pay them!

But, did I not say I would not take advantage? I will not. I will even remind you of your children; to whom I, alas! could only show at present the *affection* of a father.

M. weighs us in the scales. If gratitude out-balance love—so.

If you command it, I swear by love, I'll join my regiment to-morrow.

If love prevail, and insist upon his dues, you shall declare the victory and the prize. I *will* take no advantage.

Think over this. Neither will I take you by surprise. Sleep upon it, before you return your answer. Trim shall make the old excuse to-morrow. And, thank heaven! to-night you sleep alone.

Why did you sing that sweet song yesterday, though I so pressed you? Those words and your voice were too much.

No words can say how much I am your's.

To Mr. —

Dec. 7, 1775.

My Dear H.
Here has been a sad piece of work ever since I received your's yesterday. But don't be alarmed.—We are not discovered to the prophane. Our tender tale is only known to— (whom does your fear suggest?)—to love and gratitude, my H. And they ought both, for twenty reasons, to be *your* friends, I am sure.

They have been trying your cause, ever since the departure of honest Trim yesterday. Love, though in my opinion

not so blind, is as good a justice as Sir John Fielding. I
argued the matter stoutly—my head on his Lordship's side
of the question, my heart on your's. At last they seemed to
say, as if the oath of allegiance, which I had taken to gratitude, at a time when, heaven knows, I had never heard of
love, should be void, and I should be at full liberty to
devote myself, body and soul, to—But call on me to-
morrow before dinner, and I'll tell you their final judgment.
This I will tell you now—love sent you the tenderest
wishes, and gratitude said I could never pay you all I owe
you for your noble letter of yesterday.

Yet—oh, my H. think not meanly of me ever for this—
Do not *you* turn advocate against me.—I will not pain
you—'tis impossible you ever should.

Come then to-morrow: and surely Omiah will not murder love! Yet I thought the other day he caught our eyes
conversing. Eyes speak a language all can understand.—
But, is a child of Nature to nip in the bud that favourite
passion which his mother Nature planted, and still tends?—
What will Oberea and her coterie say to this, Omiah, when
you return from making the tour of the globe? They'll
blackball you, depend on it.

What would Rousseau say to it, my H.?

You shall tell me to-morrow. I will not write another
word; lest conscience, who is just now looking over my left
shoulder, should snatch my pen, and scratch out *to-morrow*.

To Miss—

Huntington, Dec. 7, 1775.

My dearest soul,

I hope to heaven Trim will be able to get this to you to-
night!—Not I only, but my whole future life, shall thank
you for the dear sheet of paper I have just received. Bless-

ings, blessings—But I could write and exclaim, and offer up vows and prayers, till the happy hour arrives.

Yet, hear me M. If I have thus far deserved your love, I will deserve it still. As a proof I have not hitherto pressed you for anything conscience disapproves, you shall not do to-morrow what conscience disapproves. You shall not make me happy (oh, how supremely blest!) under the roof of your benefactor and my host. It were not honourable. Our love, the inexorable tyrant of our hearts, claims his sacrifices, but does not bid us insult his Lordship's walls with it. How civilly did he invite me to H. in October last, though an unknown recruiting officer! How politely himself first introduced me to himself! Often has the recollection made me struggle with my passion. Still it shall restrain it on this side honour.

So far from triumphing or insulting, Heaven knows—if Lord S. indeed love you, if indeed it be aught beside the natural preference which age gives to youth—Heaven knows how much I pity him. Yet, as I have either said or written before, it is only the pity I should feel for a father whose affections were unfortunately and unnaturally fixed upon his own daughter.

Were I your seducer, M. and not your lover, I should not write thus—nor should I have talked or acted, or written as I have. Tell it not in Gath, nor publish it in the streets of Askalon, lest the Philistines should be upon me. I should be drummed out of my regiment for a traitor to intrigue. And can you really imagine I think so meanly of your sex! Surely you cannot imagine I think so meanly of you. Why, then, the conclusion of your last letter but one? A word thereon.

Take men and women in the lump, the villainy of these and the weakness of these—I maintain it to be less wonderful that an hundred or so should fall in the world, than that even one should stand. Is it strange the serpent conquered Eve? The devil against a woman is fearful odds.

He has conquered men, women's conquerors; he has made even angels fall.

Oh, then, ye parents, be merciful in your wrath. Join not the base betrayers of your children—drive not your children to the bottom of the precipice, because the villains have driven them half way down, where (see, see!) many have stopped themselves from falling further by catching hold of some straggling virtue or another which decks the steep-down rock. Oh, do not force their weak hands from their hold—their last, last hold! The descent from crime is natural, perpendicular, headlong enough of itself—do not increase it.

"Can women, then, no way but backward fall?"

Shall I ask your pardon for all this, M? No, there is no occasion, you say.

But to-morrow, for *to-morrow* led me out of my strait path over this fearful precipice, where I, for my part, trembled every step I took lest I should topple down headlong. Glad am I to be once more on *plain* ground again with my M.

To-morrow, about eleven, I'll be with you; but let me find you in your riding-dress and your mare ready. I have laid a plan, to which neither honour nor delicacy (and I always consult both before I propose anything to *you*) can make the least objection. This once, trust to me—I'll explain all to-morrow. Pray be ready in your *riding-dress!* Need I add, in that you know I think becomes you most? No—love would have whispered that.

Love shall be of our party—He shall not suffer the cold to approach you—he shall spread his wings over your bosom—he shall nestle in your dear arms—he shall—

When will to-morrow come? What torturing dreams must I not bear to-night!

I send you some lines which I picked up somewhere—I forget where. But I don't think them much amiss.

To paint my Celia, I'd devise
Two summer suns, in place of eyes;
Two lunar orbs should then be laid
Upon the bosom of the maid;
Bright Berenice's auburn hair
Should, where it ought, adorn my fair;
Nay all the signs in Heaven should prove
But tokens of my wondrous love.
All, did I say? Yes, all save one—
Her yielding waist should want a Zone.

To the Same.

Huntingdon, Dec. 8, 1775.

Then I release my dearest soul from her promise about to-day. If you do not see that all which he can claim by gratitude, I doubly claim by love; I have done, and will for ever have done. I would purchase my happiness at any price, but at the expense of your's.

Look over my letters, think over my conduct, consult your own heart, and read these two long letters of your writing, which I return you. Then, tell me whether we love or not. And—if we love (as witness both our hearts)—shall gratitude, *cold* gratitude, bear away the heavenly prize that's only due to love like our's? Shall my right be acknowledged, and must he possess the casket? Shall I have your soul, and shall he have your hand, your eyes, your bosom, your lips, your—

Gracious God of Love! I can neither write nor think. Send one line, half a line to

Your own, own

H.

To Mr. H—

H., 10 Dec. 75.

Your two letters of the day before yesterday, and what you said to me yesterday in my dressing-room, have drove me mad. To offer to sell out, and take the other step to get money for us both, was not kind. You know how such tenderness distracts me. As to marrying me, that you should not do upon any account. Shall the man I value be pointed at and hooted for selling himself to a Lord, for a commission or some such thing, to marry his cast mistress? My soul is above my situation.—Besides, I will not take advantage, Mr. H. of what may be only perhaps (excuse me) a youthful passion. After a more intimate acquaintance with me of a week or ten days, your opinion of me might very much change. And yet—you *may* love as sincerely as I—

But I will transcribe you a song which I don't believe you ever heard me sing, though it's my favourite. It is said to be an old Scotch ballad—nor is it generally known that Lady A.L. wrote it. Since we have understood each other, I have never sung it before you, because it is so descriptive of our situation—how much more so since your cruelly-kind proposal of yesterday! I wept, like an infant, over it this morning.

When the sheep are in fold, and the cows are at home,
And all the weary world to rest is gone,
The woes of my heart fall in showers from mine e'e
While my good man lays sound by me.

Young Jamie lov'd me well, and he sought me for his bride,
He had but a crown, he had no more beside;
To make the crown a pound, young Jamie went to sea,
And the crown and the pound, were both for me.

He had na been gone but a year and a day,
When my father broke his arm, and our cow was stole away;

When my mother she fell sick, and my Jamie at the sea,
And auld Robin Gray came wooing to me.

My father could na work, and my mother could na spin,
I toiled night and day, but their bread I could na win;
And Rob maintin'd them both, and, with tears in his e'e,
Said, "Jenny, for their sakes, oh! marry me."

My heart if said No, and I wish'd for Jamie back,
But the wind it blew sore, and his ship prov'd a wreck;
His ship prov'd a wreck: ah! why did not Jenny dee?
Why was she left to cry—"Woe is me!"

My father argu'd sore, though my mother did na speak;
She look'd in my face till my heart was fit to break;
So auld Robin got my hand—but my heart was in the sea,
—And now Robin Gray is good man to me.

I had na been a wife but of weeks only four.
When sitting right mournfully at my own door,
I saw my Jamie's ghost, for I could not think 'twas he,
Till he said, "Jenny, I'm come home to marry thee."

Sore did we weep, and little did we say,
We took but one kiss—then tore ourselves away;
I wish I was dead, but I am not like to dee,
But long shall be left to cry—"Woe is me!"

I gang like a ghost, and I do not care to spin,
I fain would think on Jamie, but that would be a sin;
I must e'en do my best a good wife to be,
For auld Robin Gray has been kind to me.

My poor eyes will only suffer me to add, for God's sake,
let me see my *Jamie* to-morrow. Your name also is Jamie.

To Mr. H—

H. 23 Feb. 76.

Where was you this morning, my life? I should have been
froze to death I believe with the cold, if I had not been waiting for *you*. I am uneasy, very uneasy. What could prevent
you? Your own appointment too. Why not write, if you
could not come?—Then, I had a dream last night, a sad
dream, my H.

. . . For thee I fear, my love;
Such ghastly dreams last night surprized my soul.

You may reply, perhaps, with my favourite Iphis,

"Heed not these black illusions of the night,
The mockings of unquiet slumbers."

Alas, I cannot help it. I am a weak woman, not a soldier.

I thought you had a duel with a person whom we have
agreed never to mention. I thought you killed each other. I
not only saw his sword, I heard it pass through my H's
body. I saw you both die; and with you, love and gratitude.
Who is there, thought I, to mourn for M?—Not one!

You may call me foolish; but I am uneasy, miserable,
wretched! Indeed, indeed I am. For God's sake, let me hear
from you.

To the Same

H. 24 Feb. 76.

That business, as I told you it would last night, obliges him
to go to town. I am to follow, for the winter. Now, my H.
for the royal black bob and the bit of chalk; or for any better
scheme you'll plan. Let me know, to-morrow, where you

think Lady G's scheme will be most practicable on the road, and there I'll take care to stop. I take my bible oath I won't deceive you, and more welcome shall you be to my longing arms than all the dukes or princes in Christendom. If I am not happy for one whole night in my life, it will not be your fault.

Is not this kind and thoughtful? Why did it never occur to you, so often as we have talked of my being obliged to leave this dear place? To me *most* dear, since it has been the scene of my acquaintance, my happiness, with H.

But, am I to leave behind me that dearest H? Surely your recruiting business must be nearly over now. You *must* go to town. Though things can't often be contrived at the A. they may—they *may*?—they *shall* happen elsewhere.

Fail not to-morrow, and do not laugh at me any more about my dream. If it was a proof of my weakness, it was a proof also of my love.

I wish the day on which I am to set out from hence could be conjured about a month further back or so. Now, you ask *why*? Look in your last year's almanack. Was not the *shortest*-day some where about that time? Come give me a kiss for that. I am sure I deserve it.—Oh, fye, Mr. H. not twenty. You are too generous in your payments. I must insist upon returning you the overplus the next time we meet—that is to-morrow, you know.

To Miss—

Huntingdon, 26 Feb. 1776.

Why will not the wished-for day, or rather night arrive? And here, I have not seen you since I know not when—not for two whole days.

But I wrote you a long letter yesterday why it would be dangerous to meet; and all in rhyme. The beginning, I assure you, was not poetry, but truth—If the conclusion was coloured too highly, you must excuse it. The pencil of love executed it, and the sly rogue will indulge himself sometimes. Let the time come, I will convince you his pencil did not much exaggerate.

Just now I was thinking of your birth-day, about which I asked you the other day. It's droll that your's and mine should be so near together. And thus I observe thereon.

> Your poets, cunning rogues, pretend
>   That men are made of clay;
> And that the heavenly potters make
>   Some five or six a day.
>
> No wonder, M. I and you
>   Don't quite detest each other,
> Or that my soul is link'd to yours,
>   As if it were its brother:
>
> For in one year we both were made,
>   Nay almost in one day—
> So, ten to one, we both came from
>   One common heap of clay.
>
> What? If I were not cast in near
>   So fine a mold as you—
> My heart (or rather, M., *your's*)
>   Is tender, fond and true.

Corporal Trim sets off to-day for our headquarters. My plan is laid so that no discovery *can* take place. Gods, that two such souls as yours and mine should be obliged to descend to arts and plans! Were it not for your dear sake, I'd scorn to do anything I would not wish discovered.

To Mr. —

H. 27 Feb. 76.

All your plans are useless. The Corporal has made his forced
march to no purpose. The fates are unkind. It is determined
that I am to go up *post*. So, we cannot possibly be happy
together, as we hoped to have been had our own horses
drawn me up; in which case I must have slept upon the
road. I am not clear old Robin Gray will not stay and attend
me. Why cannot my Jamie? Cruel fortune! But in town we
will be happy. When, again, shall I enjoy your dear society;
as I did during that, to me at least, blessed snow? Nothing
but my dear children could prevent our going with Cook to
seek for happiness in worlds unknown. There must be some
corner of the globe where mutual affection is respected.

Do not forget to meet me. Scratch out *forget*. I know
how much you think of me. Too much for your peace, nay
for your health. Indeed, my H. You don't look well. Pray be
careful!

> *"Whatever wound thy tender health,*
> *Will kill thy M's too."*

Omiah is in good humour with me again.—What kind of
animal should a naturalist expect from a native of Otaheite
and a Huntingdonshire dairy-maid? If my eyes don't deceive
me, Mr. Omiah will give us a specimen,—Will you bring
me some book to-morrow to divert me, as I post it to
town—that I may forget, if it be possible, I am posting
from you?

To Miss —

Hockerill, 1 March, 76.

It is your strict injunction that I do not offend you by suffering my pen to speak of last night. I will not, my M. nor
should I, had you not enjoined it. You once said a nearer
acquaintance would make me change my opinion of you. It
has, I *have* changed my opinion. The more I know you, the
more chastely I think of you. Notwithstanding last night
(what a night!) and our first too, I protest to God, I think
of you with as much purity as if we were going to be
married.—You take my meaning, I am sure; because they
are the thoughts which I know you wish me to entertain to
you.

You got to town safe, I hope. *One* letter may find me
before I shall be able to leave Huntingdon, whither I return
to-day; or, at least, to Cambridge. I am a fool about Crop,
you know. And I am now more tender of him because he has
carried *you*.—How little did we think that morning we
should ever make each other so happy!

Don't forget to write, and don't forget the key, against I
come to town. As far as seeing you, I will use it sometimes;
but never for an opportunity to indulge our passion. That,
positively, shall never again happen under *his* roof. How did
we applaud each other for not suffering his walls at H. to be
insulted with the first scene of it! And how happy were we
both, after we waked from our dream of bliss, to think how
often we had acted otherwise, during the time the snow
shut me up at H. a snow as dear to me, as yourself.

My mind is torn, rent, with ten thousand thoughts and
resolutions about you and about myself.

When we meet, which shall be as we fixed, I may perhaps mention *one* idea to you.

Pray let us contrive to be together some evening that
your favourite Jephtha is performed.

Enclosed is a song which came into my hands by an accident since we parted. Neither the words nor the music, I take it, will displease you.

Adieu.

> When your beauty appears
> In its graces and airs,
> All bright as an angel new-dropp'd from the sky;
> At distance I gaze,
> And am awed by my fears,
> So strangely you dazzle my eye!

> But, when, without art,
> Your kind thoughts you impart,
> When your love runs in blushes thro' every vein;
> When it darts from your eyes,
> And it pants in your heart,
> Then I know you're a woman again.

> "There's a passion and pride
> In our sex," she replied,
> "And thus, might I gratify both, I would do;
> As an angel appear
> To all lovers beside,
> But still prove a woman to you."

To the Same

Cannon coffee-house, Charing-Cross, 17 March, 76.
No further than this can I get from you, before I assure you that every word I said just now came from the bottom of my heart. I never shall be happy, never shall be happy, never shall be in my senses, till you consent to marry me. And notwithstanding the dear night at Hockerill, and the other

which your ingenuity procured me last week in D. Street, I swear by the bliss of blisses, I never will taste it again till you are my wife.

Though you can hardly have read my last scrawl, I must pester you with another. I had ordered some dinner; but I can neither eat, nor do anything else. "Mad!"—I may be mad, for what I know. I am sure I'm wretched.

For God's sake, for my life and soul's sake, if you love me, write directly hither, or at least to-night to my lodgings, and say what is that *insuperable* reason on which you dwelt so much. "Torture shall not force you to marry me." Did you not say so? Then you hate me; and what is life worth?

Suppose you had not the dear inducement of loving me (*if* you love me! Damnation blot out that *if!*), and being adored by me—still, do you not wish to relieve yourself and me from the wretched parts we act? My soul was not formed for such meanness. To steal in at the back door, to deceive, to plot, to lie—Perdition! the thought of it makes me despise myself.

Your children—Lord S.— (if we have not been ashamed of our conduct, why have we cheated conscience all along by "He" and "His" and "Old Robin Gray?" Oh, how we have descended!) My Lord S. I say cannot but provide for your dear boys. As to your sweet little girl—I will be a father to her, as well as a husband to you. Every farthing I have I will settle on you both. I will—God knows and you shall find what I will do for you both, when I am able. Good God, what would I *not* do!

Write, write, I say write. By the living God, I will have this *insuperable reason* from you, or I will not believe you love me.

To Mr. H—

A., 17 March 76.

And does my H. think I wanted such a letter as this to finish my affliction? Oh, my dear Jamie, you know not how you distress me.

And do you imagine that I have *willingly* submitted to the artifices to which I have been obliged, for your sake, to descend? What has been *your* part, from the beginning of the piece, to *mine?* I was obliged to act even to *you.* It was my business not to let you see how unhappy the artifices to which I have submitted, made me. And that they did embitter even our happiest moments—

But fate stands between us. We are doomed to be wretched. And I, every now and then, think some terrible catastrophe will be the consequence of our connexion. "Some dire event," as Storge prophetically says in Jephtha, "hangs over our heads,"—

> "Some woful song we have to sing
> In misery extream.—o never, never
> Was my foreboding mind distress'd before
> With such incessant pangs!"

Oh, that it were no crime to quit this world like Faldoni and Teresa, and that we might be happy together in some other world, where gold and silver are unknown! By your hand I could even die with pleasure. I know I could.

"Insuperable reason." Yes, my H., there is, and you force it from me. Yet, better to tell you than to have you doubt my love; that love which is now my religion. I have hardly any God but you. I almost offer up my prayers *to* you, as well as *for* you.

Know then, if you was to marry me, you would marry some hundreds pounds worth of debts; and *that* you never shall do.

Do you remember a solemn oath you took in one of your letters, when I was down at H? and how you told me afterwards it *must* be so, because you had so solemnly sworn it?

In the same solemn and dreadful words I swear that I never will marry you, happy as it would make me, while I owe a shilling in the world. Jephtha's vow is past.

What your letter says about my poor children made me weep; but it shall not make me change my resolution.

It is a further reason why I should not.—"If I do not marry you, I do not love you!" Gracious powers of love! Does my H. say so? My *not* marrying you is the strongest proof I can give you of my love. And Heaven, you know, has heard my vow. Do *you* respect it, and never tempt me to break it—for not even *you* will ever succeed. Till I have some better portion than debts, I *never* will be your's.

Then what is to be done? you ask. Why, I'll tell you, H. Your determination to drop all particular intercourse till marriage has made us one, flatters me more than I can tell you, because it shews me your opinion of me in the strongest light; it almost restores me to my own good opinion. The copy of verses you brought me on that subject is superior to anything I ever read. They shall be thy M's morning prayer, and her evening song. While you are in Ireland—

Yes, my love, in Ireland. Be ruled by me. You shall immediately join your regiment there. You know it is your duty. In the mean-time, something may happen. Heaven will not desert two faithful hearts that love like your's and mine. There are joys; there is happiness in store for us yet. I feel there is. And (as I said just now) *while you are in Ireland,* I'll write to you *every* post, *twice* by *one* post, and I'll think of you, and I'll dream of you, and I'll kiss your picture, and I'll wipe my eyes, and I will kiss it again, and then I will weep again. And—

Can I give a stronger instance of my regard for you, or a stronger proof that you ought to take my advice, than by thus begging my only joy to leave me? I will not swear I shall survive it; but, I beseech you, go!

Fool that I am—I undo with one hand, all I do with the other. My tears, which drop between every word I write, prevent the effect of my reasoning; which, I am sure, is just.

Be a man, I say—you *are* an angel. Join your regiment; and, as sure as I love you (nothing can be *more* sure), I will recall you from what will be banishment as much to me as to you, the first moment that I can marry you with honour to myself and happiness to my H.

But, I must not write thus. Adieu!

> Ill suits the voice of love when glory calls,
> And bids thee follow Jephtha to the field.

To Miss—

Ireland, 1 July 76.

Your little billet, of the 25th of last month, was a proper reproof for the contents of one of mine. 'Till I saw the joke I was truly unhappy. If you had not written the long and kind letter the next day, which came in the same packet, I should have been miserable. Yet, I wish you happy, *most* happy; but I cannot bear the thoughts of your receiving happiness from any hands (man, woman, or child) but mine. Had my affections not been fixed, as they are unalterably, elsewhere, the wife of my *friend*, with all her charms, would never fix them. I have but two masters, Love and Honour. If I did not consider you as my wife, I would add, you know I have but *one* mistress.

A friend of mine is going to England—(happy fellow I shall think him, to be but in the same country with you)—

He will call at the Cannon coffee-house for me. Do send me, thither, the French book you mention, *Werther*. If you don't, I positively never will forgive you. Nonsense, to say it will make me unhappy, or that I shan't be able to read it! Must I pistol myself, because a thick-blooded German has been fool enough to set the example, or because a German novelist has feigned such a story? If *you* don't lend it me, I will most assuredly procure it some time or another; so, you may as well have the merit of obliging me.—My friend will send a small parcel for you to D. Street. The books I send you, because I know you have not got them, and because they are so much cheaper here. If you are afraid of emptying my purse (which, by the way, is almost worn out), you shall be my debtor for them. So, send me a note of hand, *value received*. The other things are surely not worth mentioning.

To Mr. H. —

England, 20 Aug. 76.

For God's sake! Where are you? What is the matter? Why don't you write? Are you ill? God forbid! And I am not with you to nurse you! If you are, why don't you let some-body else write to me? Better all should be discovered, than suffer what I suffer. It's more than a month since I heard from you. A month used to bring me eight or ten letters. When I grew uneasy, it was in vain, as I said in my last that I endeavoured to find your friend who brought the parcel (for I would certainly have seen him, and asked him about you). What is become of all my letters for this last month? Did you get what I returned by your friend? Do you like the purse? The book you mentioned, is just the only book you should never read. On my knees, I beg that you will never, never read it! Perhaps you have read it. Perhaps—! I am distracted.—Heaven only knows to whom I may be writing this letter!

Madam, or Sir!

If you are a woman, I think you will, if you are a man, and ever loved, I am sure you will, oblige me with one line to say what is become of Mr.—of the—regiment. Direct to Mrs—, D. Street, London.—Any person whose hands my letter may fall into, will not think this much trouble; and, if they send me good news, heaven knows how a woman, who loves, if possible, too well, will thank them.

To Miss—

Cannon coffee-house, 27 June 1777, 5 o'clock. As I want both appetite and spirits to touch my dinner, though it has been standing before me these ten minutes, I can claim no merit in writing to you. May you enjoy that pleasure in your delightful situation on the banks of the Thames, which no situation, no thing upon earth, can, in your absence afford me!

Do you ask me what has lowered my spirits to-day? I'll tell you. Don't be angry, but I have been to see the last of poor Dodd. Yes, "poor Dodd!" though his life was justly for-feited to the laws of his country. The scene was affecting—it was the first of the kind I had ever seen; and shall certainly be the last. Though, had I been in England when Peter Tolosa was deservedly executed in February, for killing Duarzey, a young French woman with whom he lived; I believe I should have attended the last moments of a man who could murder the object of his love. For the credit of my country, this man (does he deserve the name of *man?*) was a Spaniard.

Do not think I want tenderness because I was present this morning. Will you allow yourself to want tenderness, because you have been present at Lear's madness, or Ophe-lia's? Certainly not. Believe me (you *will* believe me, I am sure)—I do not make a profession of it, like George S. Your

H. is neither *artiste* nor *amateur*—nor do I, like Paoli's friend and historian, hire a window by the year, which looks upon the Grass-market at Edinburgh.

Raynall's book you have read, and admire. For its humanity it merits admiration. The Abbe does not countenance an attendant on scenes of this sort by his writings, but he does by his conduct. And I would sooner take Practice's word than Theory's. Upon my honour Raynall and Charles Fox, notwithstanding the rain, beheld the whole from the top of an unfinished house, close by the stand in which I had a place.

However meanly Dodd behaved formerly, in throwing the blame of his application to the chancellor on his wife; he certainly died with resolution. More than once to-day I have heard that resolution ascribed to his hope that his friend Hawes, the humane founder of the humane society, would be able to restore him to life. But I give him more credit. Besides, Voltaire observes that the courage of a dying man is in proportion to the number of those who are present—and St. Evremond (the friend of the French M.) discovered that *les Anglais surpassent toutes les nations a mourir.* Let me surpass all mankind in happiness, by possessing my *Ninon* for life, and I care not how I die.

Some little circumstances struck me this morning, which, however you may refuse to forgive me for so spending my morning, I am sure you would not forgive me were I to omit.—Before the melancholy procession arrived, a sow was driven into the space left for the sad ceremony, nor could the idea of the approaching scene, which had brought the spectators together, prevent too many from laughing, and shouting, and enjoying the poor animal's distress, as if they had only come to Tyburn to see a sow baited.

After the arrival of the procession, the preparation of the unhappy victim mixed something disagreeably ludicrous with the solemnity. The tenderest could not but feel it, though they might be sorry that they *did* feel it. The poor man's wig was to be taken off, and the night-cap brought for the purpose was too little, and could not be pulled on without force. Valet-de-chambres are the greatest enemies to heroes. Every guinea in my pocket would I have given that he had not worn a wig, or that (wearing one) the cap had been bigger.

At last arrived the moment of death. The driving away of the cart was accompanied with a noise which best explained the feelings of the spectators for the sufferer. Did you never observe, at the sight or relation of anything shocking, that you closed your teeth hard, and drew in your breath hard through them, so as to make a sort of hissing sound? This was done so universally at the fatal moment, that I am persuaded the noise might have been heard at a considerable distance. For my own part, I detected myself, in a certain manner, accompanying the body with the motion of my own; as you have seen people wreathing and twisting and biassing themselves, after a bowl which they have just delivered.

Not all the resuscitating powers of Mr. Hawes can, I fear, have any effect; it was so long before the mob would suffer the hearse to drive away with his body.—

Thus ended the life of Dr. Dodd. How shocking, that a man, with whom I have eaten and drunk, should leave the world in such a manner! A manner which, from familiarity, has almost ceased to shock us, except when our attention is called to a Perreau or a Dodd. How many men, how many women, how many young and, as they fancy, tender females, with all their sensibilities about them, hear the sounds, by which at this moment I am disturbed, with as much indifference as they hear muffins and matches cried along the streets! *The last dying speech and confession, birth, parentage, and education*—Familiarity has even annexed a kind of humour to the cry. We forget that it always announces the death (and what a death!) of one fellow being; sometimes of half-a-dozen, or even *more*.

A lady talks with greater concern of cattle day than of hanging day. And her maid contemplates the mournful engraving at the top of a dying speech with more indifference than she regards the honest tar hugging his sweetheart at the top of "Blackeyed Susan." All that strikes us is the ridiculous tone in which the halfpenny balladmonger singer chants the *requiem*. We little recollect that, while we are smiling at the voice of the charmer, wives or husbands (charm she never so wisely), children, parents or friends, perhaps all these and more than these, as pure from crimes as we, and purer still perhaps, are weeping over the crime and punishment of the darling and support of their lives. Still less do we at this moment (for the printer always gets the start of the hangman, and many a man has bought his own dying speech on his return to Newgate by virtue of a reprieve)—still less do we ask ourselves, whether the wretch, who, at the moment we hear this (which ought to strike us as an awful sound), finds the halter of death about his neck, and now takes the longing farewel, and now hears the horses whipped and encouraged to draw from under him for ever the cart which he now, now, now feels depart from his lingering feet—whether this wretch really deserved to die more than we. Alas! were no spectators to attend executions but those who deserve to live, Tyburn would be honoured with much thinner congregations.

Well, I have made an uncomfortable sort of a meal on tea, and now I will continue my conversation with you. *Conversation*—a plague on words, they will bring along with them ideas. This is all the conversation we must have together for some days. Have I deserved the misery of being absent from my M? To bring proofs of my love would be to bring proofs of my existence. They must end together. Oh,

M. does the chaste resolution which I have so religiously observed ever since I offered you marriage deserve no smiles from fortune? Is then my evil genius never to relent? Had I not determined to deserve that success which it is not for mortals to command, I should never have struggled with my passions as I did the first time we met after your recovery. What a struggle! The time of year, the time of day, the situation, the danger from which you were hardly recovered, the number of months since we had met, the languor of your mind and body, the bed, the every thing—Ye cold-blooded, white livered sons and daughters of chastity, have ye no praises to bestow on such a forbearance as that? Yet, when your strength failed you, and grief and tenderness dissolved you in my arms; when you reclined your cheek upon my shoulder, and your warm tears dropt into my bosom, then—who could refrain?—then—

What then, ye clay-cold hypercritics in morality?

Then—even then—"I took but one kiss, and I tore myself away."

Oh, that I could take only one look at this moment!

Your last says *the sun will shine*. Alas, I see no signs of it. Our prospects seem shut up for ever.

With regard to the stage—we will talk of it. My objections are not because I doubt your success. They are of a different kind—the objections of love and delicacy. Be not uneasy about my selling out. The step was not so imprudent. What think you of orders? More than once you know you have told me I have too much religion for a soldier. Will you condescend to be a poor parson's wife?

But I shall write to-morrow at this rate.

To the Same

—street, 2 March, 1778.

Your going out of town so suddenly has not served to mend my spirits. But I will be as merry as I can. Were I to be *very* miserable after my late miraculous adventure, I should be guilty of *sullenness* against Providence. The minute account I gave you of it last week, was, I assure you, dictated by my feelings before they had forgotten the affecting circumstances. Your observations are truly just and striking. Unpardonable as the affront which I had received appears to mortal eyes, I should not readily, I fear, have found an answer to the question of the enquiring angel, on entering the world of spirits "What brings you hither?"—

Did I not tell you o' Saturday the particulars of the poor fellow who suffered this day se'nnight for murdering Mrs. Knightly? They are singular. He was an Italian, I understand. Such a thing is not credible but of an Italian.

Mrs. Knightly's account was that on the 18th of January Ceppi came into her room, she being in bed, locked the door, sat himself in a chair, and told her he was come to do her business. She, not understanding this, asked him to let her get out of bed; which he did. He then took from his pocket two pistols. She went towards the door in order to get out, but he set his back against it. She, to appease him, told him he might stay to breakfast. He answered he would have none, but would give her a good one. She then called out to alarm the house, ran towards the bed, and said, "pray don't shoot me!" and drew up close to the curtains. He followed, and discharged the pistol; after which he threw himself across the bed and fired the other pistol at himself, which did not take effect. During this, a washerwoman ran up stairs, and with a poker broke the bottom panel of the door, through which Mrs. Knightly was drawn half-naked, and Ceppi, following, ran down stairs; but was pursued and taken. In his defence, he said, he had proposed marriage to her, but that she had refused and deserted him; that he was overcome with grief and love, and that his design was not to hurt her, but to shoot himself in her presence.

It appears, I am afraid, from all the circumstances, that,

whatever his despair meant with regard to his own life, he certainly was determined to take away her's. How unaccountably must Nature have mix'd him up! Besides the criminality and brutality of the business, the folly of it strikes *me*. What—because the person, on whom I have fixed *my* affections, has robbed me of happiness by withdrawing *her's*, shall I let her add to the injury by depriving me of existence also in this world, and of every thing in the next? In my opinion to run the chance of being murdered by the new object of her affections, or of murdering him is as little reconcileable to common sense as to common religion. How much less so to commit complicated murder, which must cut off all hopes in all worlds.

Yet, could I believe (which I own I cannot, from the evidence in this case), that the idea of destroying her never struck him till his finger was at the trigger—that his only intention was to lay the breathless body of an injured lover at her feet—Had this been the fact, however I might have condemned the deed, I certainly should have wept over the momentary frenzy which committed it. But, as nothing appears to have past which could at all make him change his plan, I must (impossible as it seems) suppose him to have deliberately formed so diabolical a plan—and must rejoice that he was not of the same country, while I lament that he was of the same order of beings, with myself.

If the favour I mentioned to you o' Saturday be at all out of course, pray don't ask it. Yet the worthy veteran I want to serve has now and then seen things happen not altogether *in* course. When he called this morning to learn how I succeeded, I observed to him, while we were talking, that he got bald. "Yes," said her, shaking his grey hairs, "it will happen so by people's continually stepping over one's head."

He little suspected the channel of my application, but he asked me this morning whether 50l. if he could scrape

it together, properly slid into Miss R——'s hand, might
not forward his views. My answer was, that I had no
acquaintance with the lady, but I knew *for certain* that she
had never in her life soiled her fingers with the smallest
present of this sort.

Happy, blest, to know you, to love you, and be loved
by you!

To the Same

Hockerill, 5 Sept. 1778.

Here did I sit, more than two years ago, in this very room,
perhaps in this very chair, thanking you for bliss, for para-
dise, all claim to which I soon after voluntarily resigned,
because I hoped they would soon be mine by claims more
just, if possible, than those of love. Two years—how have I
borne existence all the while! But delicacy and respect for
you enjoined forbearance. And hope led me on from day to
day, deceiving time with distant prospects which I thought
at hand. When will the tedious journey end? When shall I
sleep away my fatigues on the down-soft pillow of the
bosom of love? Should hope continue to deceive me, you
never shall make me happy, till you make me your husband.
Yet, as we sate upon the grass, under the trees near the
water, yesterday, just before you returned me my stick,
because you thought the gentleman coming along the path
by the mill was a certain person—yet, had I then loosened
another button or two of my favourite habit, which was
already opened by the heat; had I then (you remember, my
Laura, the conversation and scene) forgotten my resolution,
forgotten every thing, and riotted in all your glowing
charms, which only love like mine could withstand—who is
he that would dare to blame me? Who would dare to say I
had done what he would not have done? But the scene must
be shifted.—Sally Harris, you know, arrived only at the dig-

nity of Pomona at Hockerill. Had my M. her due, mankind at large would admit her double claim to the titles of Minerva and of Venus.

To sleep here is impossible. As well expect the miser to sleep in a place where he once hung in raptures over a hidden treasure which is now lost. This letter I have an opportunity to send to our old friend, for you, without taking it to town. Let me fill up the remainder of my paper with an almost incredible anecdote I learned from a gentleman who joined me on this road this morning and travelled some miles with me. It happened last week, I think. Peter Ceppi you remember. Surely that Providence which prevents the propagation of monsters, does not suffer such *monstrous* examples as these to propagate.

One Empson, a footman to Dr. Bell, having in vain courted for some time a servant belonging to Lord Spencer, at last caused the banns to be put up at church, without her consent, which she forbade. Being thus disappointed, he mediated revenge; and having got a person to write a letter to her, appointing a meeting, he contrived to way-lay her, and surprise her in Lord Spencer's park. On her screaming, he discharged a pistol at her, and made his escape. The ball wounded her, but not mortally.

Oh love, love canst thou not be content to make fools of thy slaves, to make them miserable, to make them what thou pleasest! Must thou also goad them on to crimes! Must thou also convert them into devils, hell-hounds!

To the Same

————street, 28 Jan. 1779.

The short note I wrote to you last night, immediately on my reaching town, you received I hope. But why no answer to it? Why do you not say when we shall meet? I have ten thousand things to tell you. My situation in Norfolk is lovely. Exactly what you like. The parsonage house may be made very comfortable at a trifling expence. How happily shall we spend our time there! How glad am I that I have taken orders, and what obligations have I to dear B. to Mr. H. and Dr. V! Now my happiness can be deferred no longer. My character and profession are, now, additional weights in the scale. Oh then, consent to marry me directly. The day I lead you to the altar will be the happiest day of my existence.

Thanks, a thousand thanks for your tender and affectionate letters while I was in Norfolk. Be assured G. could mean nothing by what she said. She is our firm friend, I am persuaded. About an hour ago I called there; but she was out. Presently I shall go again with this, in the hope of hearing something about you.

Oh M! every day I live I do but discover more and more how impossible it is for me to live without you.

Do not forget the 5th of next month. We *must* keep that day sacred together.

To the Same

1 March, 1779.

Though we meet to-morrow, I must write you two words to-night, just to say, that I have all the hopes in the world that ten days at the utmost, will compleat the business. When that is done, your only objection is removed, along with your debts; and we may, surely, then be happy, and be so *soon*. In a month, or *six weeks at furthest*, from this time, I might certainly call you mine. Only remember that my *character* now I have taken orders, makes expedition necessary. By to-night's post I shall write into Norfolk about the alterations at *our* parsonage.—To-morrow.—G's friendship is more than I can ever return.

NOTES

1: *Why Vainly Seek to Flee? Love Will Pursue You.*

1. Cradock, *Memoirs,* vol. 1, p. 143; and Baron-Wilson, *M. G. Lewis,* vol. 1, pp. 19–20, who offers an occult interpretation of Martha's anxiety. Shortly before Martha left the Admiralty for Covent Garden Theatre, a red rose, which she wore on her dress, fell to the floor. "As she picked it up, the red leaves scattered themselves on the carpet, and the stalk alone remained in her hands. The poor girl, who had been depressed in spirits before, was evidently affected by this incident, and said, in a slightly faltering voice, 'I trust I am not to consider this as an evil omen.'"

2. Cradock, *Memoirs,* vol. 1, p. 143.

3. *Annual Register,* 1779, pp. 198–99.

4. Walpole, *Last Journals,* vol. 2, p. 248.

5. *Westminster Magazine,* April 1779, p. 171.

6. For Martha's diamond cross, see a letter to *Town and Country Magazine,* April 1779, p. 181.

7. Blunt, *Mrs. Montagu,* vol. 2, p. 70.

8. For the route taken by Martha Ray to Covent Garden and for many other incidental details in this chapter, see Dawes, *Case and Memoirs,* several editions, passim; and *Old Bailey Sessions Papers,* 16 April 1779.

9. *General Evening Post,* 8–10 April 1779.

10. *Old Bailey Sessions Papers,* 16 April 1779, p. 207.

11. Ibid.

12. Musty, "Love and Madness," p. 424.

13. *Old Bailey Sessions Papers,* 16 April 1779, pp. 209–10.

14. Quoted in Dudden, *Henry Fielding,* vol. 2, p. 736.

15. Cradock, *Memoirs,* vol. 1, pp. 145–46; and *General Evening Post,* 8–10 April 1779.

16. Martelli, *Jemmy Twitcher,* p. 177; and Moorman, *William Wordsworth,* vol. 1, pp. 260–61. Basil's feelings about his mother's murder can be gauged from the fact that throughout his long life he was "always concerned to construct laws that would regulate the passions." See Wu, "Montagu's Manuscripts," p. 251. In 1798 Basil's friend William Wordsworth wrote a poem that made use of Martha's name, yet portrayed her namesake as a probable infanticide. Entitled "The Thorn," it was published in *Lyrical Ballads.* How Basil responded to this reprehensible poem is unknown. Over time, the poem has inspired a good deal of scholarly hand-wringing.

17. For the list of jurors, see Hackman indictment in the London Metropolitan Archives.

18. *Morning Chronicle,* 10 April 1779.

19. *Morning Post,* 10 April 1779.

20. *General Evening Post,* 8–10 April 1779.

21. Ibid.

2: First Lady of the Admiralty

1. Cradock, *Memoirs,* vol. 1, p. 118.

2. For instance, see *Public Advertiser,* 10 April 1779; *Gazetteer, and New Daily Advertiser,* 12 April 1779; April editions of *Town and*

Country Magazine and *Westminster Magazine*; and the anonymous *Case and Memoirs of Miss Martha Reay*. The latter publication takes issue with Manasseh Dawes's *Case and Memoirs* for establishing the "reputation of Mr. Hackman on the ruin of Miss Reay's" (p. 14). None of these sources is unimpeachable, of course, but the information in the article in *Westminster Magazine* is based on the "most indisputable authority" (p. 171).

3. *Gazetteer, and New Daily Advertiser,* 12 April 1779; *Town and Country Magazine,* April 1779, pp. 179–80; and the St. Paul's Covent Garden Rate Books.

4. *Westminster Magazine,* April 1779, p. 171.

5. Ibid.

6. Rodger, *Insatiable Earl,* pp. 80, 85.

7. Boswell, *London Journal,* p. 52.

8. Ibid., pp. 51–52.

9. Rodger, *Insatiable Earl,* p. 7.

10. West, "Libertinism," pp. 81–91.

11. Quoted in Rodger, *Insatiable Earl,* p. 81.

12. *An Essay on Woman on Other Pieces,* p. 68. Wilkes, incidentally, may be the true author of the quip often attributed to the actor Samuel Foote. "Foote and Lord Sandwich were abusing each other in joke, when Lord Sandwich said he should like to know whether Foote would die by the pox or the gallows. To which Foote answered, 'That will happen according as I embrace your mistress or your principles.'" See Connell, *Portrait of a Whig Peer,* pp. 107–98.

13. Rodger, *Insatiable Earl,* pp. 102–4.

14. Ibid., pp. 8–9, 70–72.

15. *Town and Country Magazine,* April 1779, p. 180.

16. See Martha's letter to Sandwich, dated 24 June 1772. Mapperton Mss., F/55a/8.

17. Quoted in Marillier, *Eighteenth Century Romance,* pp. 17–18.

18. *Gentleman's Magazine,* April 1779, p. 210; and *Annual Register,* 1779, pp. 206–7.

19. *Westminster Magazine,* April 1779, p. 173.

20. Quoted in Rodger, *Insatiable Earl,* p. 117.

21. Cumberland and Cumberland, *Cumberland Letters,* p. 228.
22. Cradock, *Memoirs,* vol. 1, p. 117.
23. Mapperton Mss., F/55b/12.
24. Ibid., F/55b/13.
25. Baron-Wilson, *M. G. Lewis,* vol. 1, pp. 21–22.
26. *Town and Country Magazine,* April 1779, p. 180. The author of this article describes Galli as part of a "coterie," with Giulia Frasi, Elizabeth Pope, and Mrs. Courage. "Every one of these ladies had at times afforded gratification to Lord S——'s desires, as well in an amorous as in an harmonious manner; and some of them had borne him children, particularly Signora Fr——si."
27. Solander, *Collected Correspondence,* p. 74.
28. Burney, *Early Journals,* vol. 2, p. 44.
29. Cradock, *Memoirs,* vol. 1, pp. 126–27.
30. Quoted in McCormick, *Omai,* p. 168.
31. For Mrs. Berkeley and her friendship with Martha Ray, see the correspondence at Mapperton, in particular a letter from "P——v——a," dated 28 December 1774, F/55d/1. According to Joseph Cradock, Mrs. Berkeley was "well acquainted with all [the] particulars" of Martha's relationship with Hackman. "Mrs. Berkeley, after the death of Miss Ray, had the care of a trusty department at Somerset-house, where I had a long conference with her; but in the course of her recital she became so dreadfully agitated, that I entreated her to desist; and though I had a letter and a friendly invitation, to visit her afterwards, I confess I had been so much hurt at what had passed, that I avoided a second interview." See Cradock, *Memoirs,* vol. 1, p. 144.
32. Mapperton Mss., F/55b/20.
33. Ibid., F/55b/22.
34. William Augustus Miles to David Garrick, 15 March 1775, Garrick, *Letters,* vol. 3, p. 995. See also the letter from "P——v——a," who writes of Sandwich's "parade about the insignificancy" of Martha Ray regarding naval appointments. See Mapperton Mss., F/55d/1.
35. Sir William Gordon to Lord Sandwich, 25 August 1775, Mapperton Mss., F/55b/15.

36. 11 September 1766, Mapperton Mss., F/55a/1.

37. For instance, 6 October 1766, ibid., F/55a/6.

38. 2 October 1766, ibid., F/55a/5. It is possible that Martha had already appeared at Covent Garden Theatre by this time. See *Gazetteer, and New Daily Advertiser,* 12 April 1779: "It is well known that Miss Ray . . . sung at Covent-garden theatre when she was but fifteen."

39. 6 October 1766, ibid., F/55a/6.

40. 27 October 1766, ibid., F/55b/3.

41. Ibid., F/55a/7.

42. 20 November 1766, ibid., F/55b/4.

43. 10 September 1775, ibid., F/55b/16.

44. 24 June 1772, ibid., F/55a/8.

45. See Martha's letter to Sandwich, dated 17 October 1772, ibid., F/55a/9.

46. 22 October 1772, ibid., F/55a/10.

47. 22 October 1772, Huntington Mss., LO 9203.

48. 24 October 1772, Mapperton Mss., F/55a/11.

49. 26 October 1772, ibid., F/55a/12.

50. See Reynolds's letters to Sandwich, 26, 28, and 29 October 1772, ibid. F/55b/7–9. In his letter of 26 October Reynolds emphasized the importance of drawing Martha away from London. "I need not observe to your Lordship you will gain a very material Point in getting her out of Town."

51. 28 October 1772, ibid., F/55a/13.

52. 30 October 1772, ibid., F/55b/10.

53. Cradock, *Memoirs,* vol. 1, p. 143.

3: *The Romantic Redcoat*

1. Cradock, *Memoirs,* vol. 1, p. 141.

2. *Morning Chronicle,* 9 April 1779; and *Gazetteer, and New Daily Advertiser,* 13 April 1779.

3. *Case and Memoirs of Miss Martha Reay,* p. 10.

4. *General Evening Post,* 8–10 April 1779.

5. *Town and Country Magazine,* April 1779, p. 181; and *General Evening Post,* 13–15 April 1779.

6. Musty, "Love and Madness," p. 424.

7. *Town and Country Magazine,* April 1779, p. 181.

8. *Gazetteer, and New Daily Advertiser,* 13 April 1779; and *General Evening Post,* 13–15 April 1779.

9. White, *Story of Gosport,* p. 77.

10. Ibid.

11. *Gentleman's Magazine,* 1751, p. 400.

12. Marsh, *John Marsh Journals,* p. 35.

13. Ibid., p. 36.

14. Ibid.

15. Quoted in Vivien, "John Andre," part 2, p. 63.

16. Annual Inspections, Public Record Office, WO 27/27.

17. 68th Regiment of Foot Monthly Returns, Public Record Office, WO 17/189.

18. Annual Inspections, Public Record Office, WO 27/30.

19. T. Simes, *Military Guide,* quoted in Curtis, *Organization of the British Army,* p. 165.

20. An unnamed Belfast newspaper, quoted in Ward, *Faithful,* p. 55.

21. Dawes, *Case and Memoirs,* 8th ed., p. 2.

22. Ibid., p. 3.

23. See "Captain" Hackman's tailoring bills in the archives of the Gallery of Costume, Manchester, England.

24. Quoted by John Musty from a document in his possession, Musty, "Love and Madness," p. 424.

25. See "Mr Galli's declaration to Ld Sandwich april 8th 1779," Mapperton Mss., F/55c/3. "Mr Hackman has declared to Captain Walsingham upon the word of a dying man, that he has never spoke to Miss Ray since the beginning of the years 1776, at which time he had proposed marriage & was rejected."

26. Musty, "Love and Madness," p. 424, quoting Booth's account book under date 5 March 1776. "At Slaurs [Slaughter's Coffee House] in Eveng with Capt. Hackman when he sett off for Ireland 0.1.0."

4: *Love and Madness*

1. Jones, *Diary,* p. 158.
2. *General Evening Post,* 15–17 April 1779.
3. Enoch and Threthowan, *Uncommon Psychiatric Syndromes,* p. 17.
4. Burton, *Anatomy of Melancholy,* part 3, sec. 2, p. 41.
5. Boswell, writing in *London Magazine,* October 1778, p. 459.
6. Quoted in Jackson, *Melancholia and Depression,* p. 355.
7. Quoted in Small, *Love's Madness,* p. 8.
8. Quoted in Jackson, *Melancholia and Depression,* pp. 356–57.
9. Quoted in Small, *Love's Madness,* pp. 6–7.
10. Battie, *Treatise on Madness,* p. 37.
11. Cullen and Gaub, both quoted in Jackson, *Melancholia and Depression,* pp. 367, 368.
12. Thomson, *Seasons,* p. 50.
13. Partridge, *Three Wartons,* pp. 164, 166.
14. See Barker-Benfield, *Culture of Sensibility,* passim.
15. Quoted in Small, *Love's Madness,* p. 12.
16. For Faldoni and Theresa, see McManners, *Death and the Enlightenment,* p. 422; and Angelo, *Reminiscences,* vol. 2, pp. 396–400.
17. *Old Bailey Sessions Papers,* 21 February 1778, pp. 132, 134.
18. Quoted in Doughty, "English Malady," p. 259.
19. Cheyne, *English Malady,* dedication.
20. Quoted in Doughty, "English Malady," p. 261.
21. Quoted in Bartel, "Suicide," p. 145.
22. *General Evening Post,* 8–10 April 1779.
23. Ibid., 17–20 April 1779.
24. Georg Christoph Lichtenberg, quoted in Bartel, "Suicide," p. 145.
25. Quoted in Long, "Goethe's Werther," p. 170.
26. *Public Advertiser,* 30 April 1779.
27. Goethe, *The Sorrows of Werter,* vol. 2, pp. 125–27.
28. Norwich Benefice Lists, Public Record Office, E331 Norwich 38; and "Letter from Mr. Hackman to Miss Ray," Dawes, *Case and Memoirs,* 6th ed., pp. 29–30. Hackman's ordination papers were wit-

nessed by three clerics: Charles Este, a "Reading Chaplain" at Whitehall; Francis Hume, a vicar and usher at Westminster School; and William Rugge, the rector of Buckland, near Dorking in Surrey. See Norwich Diocesan Archives, Norfolk Public Record Office, DN/ORD 10. Este was the most distinguished of these men. Described by writer John Taylor as one of the "most extraordinary" characters of the age, he was a relation of one of Hackman's army colleagues. Later, he wrote theatrical criticisms for the *Public Advertiser* and played an important role in the life of *The World,* a very successful London newspaper. See Taylor, *Records of My Life,* vol. 2, p. 289.

29. At least, according to Manasseh Dawes. See a copy of his anonymous letter to Signora Galli, Mapperton Mss., F/55c/12. In the letter, Dawes offered to collaborate with Galli on a pamphlet vindicating her of behaving "improperly" in respect to Martha Ray and Hackman. Galli, however, refused to cooperate.

30. Dawes, *Case and Memoirs,* 6th ed., pp. 29–31. For an opinion challenging the authenticity of this letter, see *Westminster Magazine,* April 1779, p. 186. Compare also James Boswell's remark in *St. James's Chronicle,* 15–17 April 1779: "[Hackman] never once attempted to have a licentious connexion with Miss Ray." I have quoted extensively from Boswell's letter in chap. 8.

31. Mapperton Mss., F/55c/3.

32. *Old Bailey Sessions Papers,* 16 April 1779, p. 209.

33. Dawes, *Case and Memoirs,* 9th ed., pp. 15–16. Later, one writer explained Galli's words to Hackman on the grounds that she had herself fallen in love with him; and "from the frequent presents she received from him, was flattered into a belief that their inclinations were mutual." See *Nocturnal Revels,* vol. 1, p. 247.

34. The letter is endorsed "This anonimous letter letter [*sic*] Mr Hackman acknowledged to Captain Walsingham to be written by him." Mapperton Mss., F/55b/19.

35. See Walsingham's letter to Sandwich, ibid., F/55c/5.

36. *General Evening Post,* 8–10 April 1779.

37. *See* Sandwich's letter to his solicitor, William Chetham, dated 15 April 1779, Mapperton Mss., F/55c/9.

5: *Sensation*

1. Quoted in Jesse, *George Selwyn,* vol. 4, p. 66.
2. Walpole, *Correspondence,* vol. 33, p. 98.
3. Ibid., p. 101.
4. Ibid., vol. 2, p. 156.
5. Quoted in Jesse, *George Selwyn,* vol. 4, p. 76.
6. Ibid., p. 75.
7. *General Evening Post,* 8–10 April 1779; and *Gazetteer, and New Daily Advertiser,* 12 April 1779.
8. *Morning Chronicle,* 9 April 1779.
9. Ibid.
10. *Westminster Magazine,* April 1779, pp. 173, 213.
11. *Gazetteer, and New Daily Advertiser,* 17 April 1779. See appendix 1 for the full text of the poem.
12. Lennox, *Life and Letters,* p. 296.
13. *Morning Chronicle,* 7 May 1779. For the full texts of Sabrina's letters, see appendix 4. Some of the public's sympathy for Hackman's plight may have been motivated by dislike of Lord Sandwich. See, for instance, remarks of artist and republican James Barry, as paraphrased by Henry Angelo. Barry, he writes, used to speak of Hackman's "unfortunate fate with great sympathy, and never failed to let loose the most violent epithets against the titled *baist,* as he designated the gay old peer, her protector, the renowned *Jemmy Twitcher.*" See Angelo, *Reminiscences,* vol. 1, p. 378.
14. *Morning Post,* 10 April 1779.
15. Quoted in Howson, *Macaroni Parson,* p. 66.
16. Ibid., p. 118.
17. Ibid., p. 135.
18. Ibid., p. 153.

19. Ibid., p. 154.
20. Angelo, *Reminiscences,* vol. 1, p. 354.
21. Quoted in Howson, *Macaroni Parson,* p. 210.
22. Ibid., pp. 207–8.
23. Mapperton Mss., F/55c/1.
24. *Gazetteer, and New Daily Advertiser*, 12 April 1779.
25. Mapperton Mss., F/55c/3. For other versions of Mr. Galli's declaration, see Mapperton Mss., F/55c/2; and British Library, Additional Mss., 35,615, f.204.
26. 9 April 1779, Mapperton Mss., F/55c/6.
27. *Gazetteer, and New Daily Advertiser,* 12 April 1779. One writer called Sandwich's decision to bury Martha in the clothes in which she was "assassinated" an "unaccountable caprice." See *Town and Country Magazine*, April 1779, p. 181. The writer adds that Martha's watch, "which was much damaged in her fall," and a diamond cross were removed before her burial.
28. *General Evening Post,* 8–10 April 1779.
29. Ibid.
30. *Morning Chronicle*, 10 April 1779.
31. *General Evening Post,* 8–10 April 1779.
32. Mapperton Mss., F/55c/7.
33. Barnes and Owen, *Private Papers*, vol. 2, p. 258.
34. Blunt, *Mrs. Montagu*, vol. 2, p. 70; and *Gazetteer, and New Daily Advertiser,* 15 May 1779.
35. Walpole, *Correspondence,* vol. 2, p. 156n.

6: *Newgate Prison*

1. *Gazetteer, and New Daily Advertiser,* 12 April 1779.
2. *General Evening Post,* 8–10 April 1779.
3. Linebaugh, *London Hanged*, pp. 30–37, specifically on Jack Sheppard.
4. Quoted in W. J. Sheehan, "Finding Solace in Eighteenth-Century Newgate," in J. S. Cockburn, *Crime in England*, p. 229.

5. Boswell, *London Journal,* pp. 251–52.

6. Kalman, "Newgate Prison," pp. 51, 55–56.

7. Quoted in Babington, *English Bastille,* p. 102.

8. Howard, *State of the Prisons,* p. 162.

9. Ibid., p. 161.

10. Gatrell, *Hanging Tree,* p. 383. For a more positive assessment of Villette, see Boswell's remark in Birkbeck Hill's edition of Boswell's *Life of Johnson:* "His extraordinary diligence is highly praiseworthy, and merits a distinguished reward" (vol. 4, p. 380).

11. W. J. Sheehan, "Finding Solace, in Eighteenth-Century Newgate," in J. S. Cockburn, *Crime in England,* pp. 239–40.

12. *General Evening Post,* 13–15 April 1779.

13. *Gazetteer, and New Daily Advertiser,* 12 April 1779.

14. *General Evening Post,* 13–15 April 1779.

15. Delany, *Autobiography,* vol. 2, p. 424.

16. *General Evening Post,* 13–15 April 1779.

17. *European Magazine,* February 1782, p. 125.

18. For the identification of Dawes as the author of *Case and Memoirs,* see G. Burgess's edition of Herbert Croft's *Love and Madness,* p. xiv, and the *Public Advertiser,* 2, 5 June 1779. On June 2 the paper printed the following poem: "The Rope, the Penalty of broken Laws,/Is not more *shocking* than the pen of D—— WS./Both to deserve, no Crime can be so great;/Yet both to suffer was poor Hackman's Fate." In the *Case,* Dawes implied that Frederick Booth had authorized his pamphlet: "What I have written comes from Mr. Hackman, his brother-in-law, the closet, and the heart." (*Case and Memoirs,* 8th ed., no page number). But Booth published a series of advertisements denying it. See, for instance, *Public Advertiser,* 13 April 1779. Dawes dedicated his book to Lord Sandwich.

19. *European Magazine,* February 1782, p. 125.

20. Dawes, *Case and Memoirs,* 6th ed., p. xi.

21. Ibid., pp. ix–x.

22. Booth's absorption in Hackman's affairs can be deduced from his daybook for 1779, Westminster City Archives, Frederick Booth Papers, 36/15.

23. *Public Advertiser,* 12 April 1779. According to rumor, Mary Booth later went "mad." See Mary Townshend's letter to George Selwyn, dated 27 April 1779. "That would account, if true, in some measure for his [Hackman's] action," Miss Townshend added. Jesse, *George Selwyn,* vol. 4, p. 99.

24. *Old Bailey Sessions Papers,* 16 April 1779, p. 209.

25. Ibid.

26. Walker, *Crime and Insanity,* pp. 36–37.

27. Joel Peter Eigen, "Intentionality and Insanity," in W. F. Bynum, et al., *The Anatomy of Madness,* pp. 37–39.

28. Walpole, *Correspondence,* vol. 21, p. 396.

29. *Newgate Calendar,* p. 181.

30. Ibid., p. 183.

31. Douglas Hay, "Property, Authority and the Criminal Law," in Hay, *Albion's Fatal Tree,* pp. 33–34.

32. Quoted in Walker, *Crime and Insanity,* p. 59.

33. Ibid., p. 61.

34. Ibid., p. 62.

7: A Public Example

1. *Morning Chronicle,* 17 April 1779; and *Public Advertiser,* 19 April 1779.

2. Boswell, *Laird of Auchinleck,* p. 85. The attractive woman sitting next to Boswell at the chief prosecuting counsel's table was Mrs. Winifred Maxwell-Constable, a granddaughter of the fifth earl of Nithsdale. Lady Ossory's presence at the trial is vouched for by her letter to George Selwyn, dated 17 April 1779. Hackman's "behaviour yesterday was wonderfully touching," she writes. See Jesse, *George Selwyn,* vol. 4, pp. 74–75.

3. Langbein, "Criminal Trial," pp. 280–81.

4. *Public Advertiser,* 17 April 1779.

5. *Old Bailey Sessions Papers,* 16 April 1779, p. 207.

6. Ibid., pp. 207–8.

7. *Public Advertiser,* 17 April 1779.

8. *Old Bailey Sessions Papers*, 16 April 1779, p. 208.

9. Ibid.

10. Ibid., pp. 208–9.

11. Ibid., p. 209; and *Gazetteer, and New Daily Advertiser*, 17 April 1779. The editors of Horace Walpole's correspondence speculate that O'Bryen may have been "Dennis O'Bryen (1755–1822), a surgeon who later became a pamphleteer." See Walpole's *Correspondence,* vol. 33, p. 101. This O'Bryen was also a friend of Charles James Fox, the Whig politician.

12. *Old Bailey Sessions Papers,* 16 April 1779, p. 209.

13. Dawes, *Case and Memoirs,* 9th ed., p. 25. For Cumberland's speech, see Andrew and McGowen, *Perreaus and Mrs. Rudd,* p. 37. Dodd also turned to Cumberland as a speechwriter; "but," wrote Cumberland, "as soon as I understood that application had been made to Dr. Johnson, and that he [Dodd] was about to be taken under his shield, I did what every other friend to the unhappy would have done, consigned him to the stronger advocate." See Howson, *Macaroni Parson,* pp. 177–78.

14. Blackstone, *Commentaries,* vol. 4, p. 24.

15. *Gazetteer, and New Daily Advertiser,* 17 April 1779.

16. Ibid.

17. *Public Advertiser,* 17 April 1779.

18. *Gazetteer, and New Daily Advertiser,* 17 April 1779.

19. Ibid.

20. *Old Bailey Sessions Papers,* 16 April 1779, p. 210.

21. Quoted in Peter Linebaugh, "Tyburn Riot against the Surgeons," in Hay, *Albion's Fatal Tree,* p. 65.

22. *Gazetteer, and New Daily Advertiser,* 17 April 1779. Dawes probably wrote the *Morning Chronicle*'s account of Hackman's trial, as it contains a puff for the *Case and Memoirs.* "As the public may have curiosity to gratify, respecting the particulars of his [Hackman's] case, they are requested to suspend their opinion with pity upon it, until it shall be put before them by his friends, uninflamed by prejudice or unornamented by partiality." See *Morning Chronicle,* 17 April 1779.

8: *Boswell and Hackman*

1. Boswell, *London Journal,* p. 83. Actually, Boswell uses "nymph," singular.
2. Ibid., p. 227.
3. Boswell, *Boswell on the Grand Tour,* pp. 247–48.
4. Boswell, *Boswell in Extremes,* pp. 64–65.
5. Stone, *Family, Sex and Marriage,* p. 353.
6. Boswell, *Laird of Auchinleck,* p. 79.
7. Ibid., p. 92.
8. *Public Advertiser,* 19 April 1779.
9. Boswell, *Laird of Auchinleck,* p. 85.
10. *St. James's Chronicle,* 15–17 April 1779.
11. Boswell, *Laird of Auchinleck,* pp. 90–91. When during the same evening Boswell gave Johnson an account of Hackman's speech to the jury, Johnson commented, "I hope he shall find mercy" (ibid., p. 85).
12. Dawes, *Case and Memoirs,* 9th ed., p. 48; and Martelli, *Jemmy Twitcher,* p. 173, quoting an untraced newspaper. Sandwich's offer to procure a reprieve for Hackman may have been motivated in part by public pressure. See, for instance, the letter from "A Magistrate present at the Trial" in the *London Evening Post,* 13–15 April 1779. "I have not the honour of being personally known to the noble Earl, nor do I wish to encrease his Lordship's feelings on the melancholy occasion, which I doubt not are sufficiently poignant; but had Miss Ray been my nearest relation, I should be the first person to make application to his Lordship, and beg his kind and powerful interference (in behalf of the truly penitent Mr. Hackman) with a Prince who is full of humanity, benevolence, and mercy; and who, I am persuaded, will grant the request of the noble Earl, if he makes it in time." According to the *Gazetteer, and New Daily Advertiser,* 20 April 1779, some of Hackman's friends did approach the king in any case, "but his Majesty would not listen to the application." Devereaux, "City and the Sessions Paper," describes the appeal process, pp. 471–72.

13. See Walsingham's letter to Sandwich, Mapperton Mss., F/55c/6.
14. McLynn, *Crime and Punishment,* p. 272; and Linebagh, "Tyburn Riot," esp. pp. 115–16.
15. Quoted in Radzinowicz, *History,* vol. 1, p. 206.
16. Villette, *Genuine Life,* p. 18. Like other pamphlet accounts of prisoners' lives, trials, and dying words, *Genuine Life* is apparently based in part upon newspaper reports.

9: *This Good Old Custom*

1. For the figure of over thirteen hundred executions, see Gatrell, *Hanging Tree,* app. 2, "Execution and Mercy Statistics."
2. Wilf, "Imagining Justice," p. 51.
3. McLynn, *Crime and Punishment,* p. 264; and Grose, *Vulgar Tongue.*
4. Angelo, *Reminiscences,* vol. 1, p. 363.
5. Gatrell, *Hanging Tree,* pp. 602–3; and Wilf, "Imagining Justice," pp. 66–67, quoting Sheriff Thomas Skinner.
6. Boswell, *Boswell's Life of Johnson,* vol. 4, pp. 217–18.
7. Gatrell, *Hanging Tree,* pp. 90–97, citing T. W. Lacqueur.
8. My account of executions in this chapter is particularly indebted to Radzinowicz, *History of English Criminal Law,* chap. 6, "Execution of Capital Sentences"; and McLynn, *Crime and Punishment,* chap. 14, "Execution."
9. Quoted in McLynn, *Crime and Punishment,* p. 265.
10. Angelo, *Reminiscences,* vol. 1, pp. 368–69.
11. Walpole, *Correspondence,* vol. 21, p. 399.
12. Ibid., p. 402.
13. *Newgate Calendar,* p. 350.
14. Gatrell, *Hanging Tree,* p. 46.
15. Burke, *Romance of the Forum,* vol. 1, p. 275
16. Boswell, *London Magazine,* May 1783, p. 204. From Boswell's letter to the *Public Advertiser,* dated 25 April 1768, and republished in May 1783 as part of no. 68 of his "Hypochondriack" essays.
17. Boswell, *London Magazine,* p. 204.

18. Samuel Foote invented the term. See Angelo, *Reminiscences*, vol. 1, p. 367.

19. Jesse, *George Selwyn*, vol. 1, p. 10.

20. Ibid., p. 5.

21. Ibid. Selwyn was absent from London during the period of the Hackman case, but that didn't stop one newspaper from reporting his presence. "A correspondent says that George Selwyn, with a humanity which did honour to his feelings, out of his great esteem and respect for that amiable lady, who was so inhumanely murdered in coming out of the playhouse, attended at the Shakespeare whilst the body lay there, sitting as a mourner in the room, with a long black cloak on, which reached to his heels, and a large hat slouched over his face. This made a singular addition to a countenance naturally dark and rueful, and rendered him as complete a figure of woe as ever was exhibited at any funeral, or in any procession. It was his friend, the Duke of Q[ueensbur]y, who detected him in that garb; his Grace, by a similarity of feelings, being drawn to the same place" (ibid., vol. 4, pp. 64–65).

22. Villette, *Genuine Life,* p. 18.

23. *General Evening Post,* 17–20 April 1779.

24. Ibid. "In the chapel he [Hackman] delivered a paper to the Ordinary, the contents of which, it is hoped for the satisfaction of the public, will be laid before them; for there is evidently a *something* hangs suspended in doubt, and remains unrevealed, except Mr. Hackman has resolved the mystery to his friends."

25. Contemporary magazine or newspaper article, quoted in Jesse, *George Selwyn*, vol. 4, p. 83.

26. *General Evening Post*, 17–20 April 1779.

27. See appendix 2 for the full text of both these broadsides.

28. *General Evening Post,* 17–20 April 1779. Apparently, this was not the only fatality arising from Hackman's last hours and execution. Just as Hackman was "turned off," a "fellow who had climbed up to the top of a house where a number of people were assembled to see the execution, threw down some tiles, at the same time bawling out that the house was falling, which so terri-

fied some women in it, that they fainted away; one in particular was so greatly shocked, that notwithstanding every assistance that could be procured, she expired in a few hours." See the *Gazetteer, and New Daily Advertiser*, 20 April 1779. Other famous criminals inspired similar reports. See Andrew and McGowen, *Perreaus and Mrs. Rudd,* pp. 9–10.

29. *General Evening Post,* 17–20 April 1779.
30. Villette, *Genuine Life,* p. 19; Thrale, *Thraliana,* vol. 1, p. 385; and Boswell, *Laird of Auchinleck,* p. 93.
31. Villette, *Genuine Life,* p. 20.
32. Lord Carlisle to George Selwyn, 19 April 1779; Jesse, *George Selwyn*, vol. 4, p. 85.
33. Thrale, *Thraliana,* vol. 1, p. 386.
34. *General Evening Post,* 17–20 April 1779.
35. Boswell, *Laird of Auchinleck,* p. 93.
36. Ibid.
37. Ibid.
38. *Lloyd's Evening Post,* 16–19 April 1779, cited in Boswell, *Laird of Auchinleck,* pp. 93–94.
39. Boswell, *Laird of Auchinleck,* p. 95.
40. *Public Advertiser,* 21 April 1779.
41. Villette, *Genuine Life,* p. 21; and *General Evening Post,* 17–20 April 1779.
42. *Gazetteer, and New Daily Advertiser,* 21 April 1779.
43. Jesse, *George Selwyn,* vol. 4, p. 96.
44. Angelo, *Reminiscences,* vol. 2, p. 192.
45. *General Evening Post,* 17–20 April 1779; and Westminster City Archives, St. Martin-in-the-Fields Parish Registers, vol. 115 m/f.
46. "A Meteorological Diary of the Weather for April 1779," *Gentleman's Magazine,* March 1780.

EPILOGUE

1. Sichel, *Emma, Lady Hamilton,* p. 379; *Gentleman's Magazine,* August 1807, p. 784, and May 1831, p. 475; Westminster City Archives, index to the Frederick Booth Papers.
2. Major Arabin, quoted in Rodger, *Insatiable Earl,* p. 311.
3. Ibid.
4. Ibid., p. 313.
5. See a copy of Dawes's anonymous letter to "Mrs. Galli at Mr. Kelly's No 3. James Street Hay Market" and Galli's reply. Mapperton Mss., F/55c/12.
6. *Monthly Mirror,* quoted in Highfill, *Biographical Dictionary,* vol. 5, p. 438.
7. Mount-Edgcumb, *Musical Reminiscences,* pp. 19–20.
8. Ibid., p. 20.
9. Boswell, *London Journal,* p. 155. The arithmetic is Lawrence Stone's. See Stone, *Family, Sex and Marriage,* p. 354. Some of the outbreaks "may have been recrudescences of latent old disease rather than new infections."
10. Quoted in Brady, *James Boswell,* p. 296.
11. Ibid., p. 490.
12. Quoted in Dudden, *Henry Fielding,* vol. 2, p. 1073.
13. *Gentleman's Magazine,* 1783, p. 453.
14. Ibid.
15. *City Biography,* quoted in Vaux, *Memoirs,* p. 303. See also Gatrell, *Hanging Tree,* pp. 359–60, 509.
16. Mitford, *Sir J. Sylvester,* p. 8.
17. Lockmiller, *Sir William Blackstone,* p. 131.
18. Quoted in *Dictionary of National Biography,* vol. 2, p. 600.
19. *Daily Universal Register,* quoted in Abbott, *Lords of the Scaffold,* p. 128.
20. Ibid.

BIBLIOGRAPHY

Manuscripts

British Library
Letter from Lord Sandwich to Lord Hardwicke, 11 April 1779 (35,615, f.202)
Mr. Galli's Examination (35,615, f.204)

Gallery of Costume (Manchester, England)
James Hackman tailoring bills

Huntington Library (San Marino, California)
Letters from Lord Sandwich to Lord Loudon, 22 and 30 October 1772 (LO 9203 and LO 6241)

London Metropolitan Archives
Indictment of James Hackman (OB/SR 187)
Gaol Delivery Books (OB/RSB/2)

Mapperton (near Beaminster, Dorset)
Letters from Martha Ray to the earl of Sandwich, and one from Martha Ray to Caterina Galli (F/55a)
Correspondence relating to Martha Ray (F/55b)
Items relating to the murder of Martha Ray, including letters from Sir John Fielding and Caterina Galli (F/55c)

Miscellaneous items relating to Martha Ray, including references to the Navy Office housekeeper, Mrs. Berkeley (F/55d)

Hampshire Record Office
Proceedings of the Gosport Trustees (123M96/DTI)

Norfolk Record Office
Norwich Diocesan Archives (DN/ORD 10 and DN/ORR 3/2)

Portsmouth Records Office
Parish Registers, Holy Trinity Church, Gosport (CHU43/1A/4 and 5)

Public Record Office (Kew, England)
Lieutenants Passing Certificates (ADM 107/3)
Norwich Benefice Lists (E 331 Norwich/38)
68th Regiment of Foot Monthly Returns (WO 17/189)
68th Regiment of Foot Musters (WO 12/7622)
68th Regiment of Foot Musters (WO 12/7623)
68th Regiment of Foot Annual Inspections (WO 27/27 and 27/30)

Westminster City Archives
Frederick Booth Papers (36/13, 36/15, 36/25)
St. Martin-in-the-Fields Parish Registers: Burials (vol. 115 m/f)
St. Paul's, Covent Garden Rate Books

Broadsides

A Copy of Verses, on the Murder of the celebrated Miss Reay (1779)

The Sorrowful Lamentation and the last farewell to the world, of the Rev. James Hackman (1779)

Newspapers and Magazines

Annual Register
European Magazine
Gazetteer, and New Daily Advertiser
General Evening Post
Gentleman's Magazine
London Evening Post
London Magazine
Morning Chronicle
Morning Post
Public Advertiser
St James's Chronicle
The Times
Town and Country Magazine
Westminster Magazine

Books and Articles

Abbey, Charles J., and John H. Overton. *The English Church in the Eighteenth Century,* 2d ed., London, 1887.

Abbott, Geoffrey. *Lords of the Scaffold: A History of the Executioner.* London, 1991.

Andrew, Donna T., and Randall McGowen. *The Perreaus and Mrs. Rudd: Forgery and Betrayal in Eighteenth-Century England*. Berkeley and Los Angeles, 2001.

Angelo, Henry. *The Reminiscences of Henry Angelo*. 2 vols. London, 1904.

Babington, Anthony. *The English Bastille*. London, 1971.

Barker-Benfield, G. J. *The Culture of Sensibility: Sex and Society in Eighteenth-Century Britain*. Chicago, 1992.

Barnes, G. R., and J. H. Owen. *The Private Papers of John, Earl of Sandwich*. 4 vols. London, 1932–38.

Baron-Wilson, Margaret Cornwall (attrib.). *The Life and Correspondence of M. G. Lewis*. 2 vols. London, 1839.

Bartel, Roland. "Suicide in Eighteenth-Century England: The Myth of a Reputation." *Huntingdon Library Quarterly* 23 (1959): 145–58.

Bates, William. "The Rev. Sir Herbert Croft, Bart., LL.B." *Notes and Queries,* 4th series, no. 8 (21 October 1871), pp. 319–20.

Battie, William. *Treatise on Madness*. Edited by Richard Hunter and Ida Macalpine. London, 1962.

Beattie, J. M. "Scales of Justice: Defense Counsel and the English Criminal Trial in the Eighteenth and Nineteenth Centuries." *Law and History Review,* vol. 9, no. 2 (Fall 1991): 221–67.

Blackstone, William. *Commentaries on the Laws of England*. 4 vols. London, 1778.

Bleackley, Horace. *Ladies Fair and Frail*. London, 1925.

Blunt, Reginald. *Mrs. Montagu "Queen of the Blues."* 2 vols. London, [1923].

Boswell, James. *Boswell in Extremes, 1776–1778.* Edited by Charles McC. Weis and Frederick A. Pottle. New Haven, Conn., 1971.

————. *Boswell on the Grand Tour: Germany and Switzerland 1764.* Edited by F. Pottle. London, 1953.

————. *Boswell's London Journal 1762–1763.* Edited by F. Pottle. London, 1950.

————. *Laird of Auchinleck 1778–1782.* Edited by J. W. Reed and F. Pottle. New York, 1977.

————. *Boswell's Life of Johnson.* 6 vols. Edited by George Birkbeck Hill. New York, 1891.

Brady, Frank. *James Boswell: The Later Years 1769–1795.* London, 1984.

Burke, Peter. *The Romance of the Forum.* 2 vols. London, 1852.

Burney, Charles. *The Letters of Charles Burney 1751–1784.* Edited by Alvaro Ribeiro. Oxford, 1991.

Burney, Fanny. *The Early Journals and Letters of Fanny Burney.* 3 vols. Edited by Lars E. Troide and Stewart J. Cooke. Oxford, 1988–1994.

Burton, Robert. *The Anatomy of Melancholy.* Edited by Holbrook Jackson. New York, 1977.

Bynum, W. F., et al., eds. *The Anatomy of Madness: Essays in the History of Psychiatry.* Vol. 2. London, 1985.

The Case and Memoirs of Miss Martha Reay. Anonymous. London, 1779.

Cheyne, George. *The English Malady*. Edited by Roy Porter. London, 1991.

Cockburn, J. S., ed. *Crime in England 1550–1800*. London, 1977.

Connell, Brian. *Portrait of a Whig Peer, compiled from the papers of the Second Viscount Palmerston 1739–1802*. London, 1957.

Cradock, Joseph. *Literary and Miscellaneous Memoirs*. 4 vols. London, 1826.

Crocker, Lester G. "The Discussion of Suicide in the Eighteenth Century." *Journal of the History of Ideas* 13 (1952): 47–72.

Croft, Herbert. *Love and Madness*. London, 1780.

——. *The Love Letters of Mr. H. & Miss R. 1775–1779* (another edition of *Love and Madness*). Edited by G. Burgess. London, 1895.

Cruickshank, D., and N. Burton. *Life in the Georgian City*. London, 1990.

Cumberland, George, and Richard Cumberland. *The Cumberland Letters*. Edited by Clementina Black. London, 1912.

Cunnington, C. Willett, and Phillis Cunnington. *Handbook of English Costume in the Eighteenth Century*. London, 1957.

Curtis, Edward E. *The Organization of the British Army in the American Revolution*. New Haven and London, 1926.

Dawes, Manasseh (attrib.). *The Case and Memoirs of the late Rev. Mr. James Hackman*. 6th, 8th, and 9th eds. London, 1779.

Delany, Mary. *The Autobiography and Correspondence of Mary Granville, Mrs. Delany*. Edited by Lady Llanover. 3 vols. London, 1862.

Devereaux, Simon. "The City and the Sessions paper: 'Public Justice' in London, 1770–1800." *Journal of British Studies*, 35 (October 1996): 466–503.

The Dictionary of National Biography, edited by Sir Leslie Stephen and Sir Sidney Lee. 63 vols. London, 1885–1900.

Doughty, Oswald. "The English Malady of the Eighteenth Century." *Review of English Studies* 2, no. 7 (1926): 257–69.

Dudden, F. Homes. *Henry Fielding: His Life, Works, and Times*. 2 vols. Oxford, 1952.

Enoch, M. David, and W. H. Trethowan. *Uncommon Psychiatric Syndromes*. 2d ed. Bristol, 1979.

An Essay on Woman and Other Pieces. Anonymous. London, 1871.

Fedden, Henry Romilly. *Suicide: A Social and Historical Study*. London, 1938.

Garrick, David. *The Letters of David Garrick*. Edited by David M. Little and George M. Kharl. 3 vols. Oxford, 1963.

Gatrell, V. A. C. *The Hanging Tree: Execution and the English People 1770–1868*. Oxford, 1994.

George, M. Dorothy. *London Life in the Eighteenth Century*. London, 1925.

Gilbert, Arthur N. "Law and Honour among Eighteenth-Century British Army Officers." *Historical Journal* 19, no. 1 (1976): 75–87.

Goethe, J. W. von. *The Sorrows of Werter*. Translation attrib. to D. Malthus. 2 vols. London, 1779.

Goldberg, Brian. "Romantic Professionalism in 1800: Robert Southey, Herbert Croft, and the Letters and Legacy of Thomas Chatterton." *ELH* 63 (1996): 681–706.

Grose, Francis. *A Classical Dictionary of the Vulgar Tongue.* Edited by Eric Patridge. London, 1963.

Hay, Douglas, et al., ed. *Albion's Fatal Tree: Crime and Society in Eighteenth-Century England.* London, 1975.

Highfill, Philip H., Jr., et al. *A Biographical Dictionary of Actors, Actresses, Musicians, Dancers, Managers and other Stage Personnel in London, 1660–1800.* 16 vols. Carbondale, Ill., 1973–93.

Hogan, Charles Beecher, ed. *The London Stage 1660–1800, Part 5: 1776–1800.* Carbondale, Ill., 1968.

Houlding, J. A. *Fit for Service: The Training of the British Army, 1715–1795.* Oxford, 1981.

Howard, John. *The State of the Prisons.* Edited by K. Ruck. London, 1929.

Howson, Gerald. *The Macaroni Parson: A Life of the Unfortunate Doctor Dodd.* London, 1973.

Hume, David. *Essays: Moral, Political and Literary.* London, 1903.

Hunter, R., and I. Macalpine. *Three Hundred Years of Psychiatry 1535–1860.* London, 1963.

Jackson, Stanley W. *Melancholia and Depression from Hippocratic Times to Modern Times.* New Haven, Conn., and London, 1986.

Jesse, J. H. *George Selwyn and His Contemporaries.* 4 vols. London, 1882.

Jones, William. *The Diary of the Revd. William Jones 1777–1821.* Edited by O. F. Christie. London, 1929.

Kalman, Harold D. "Newgate Prison." *Architectual History* 12 (1969): 50–61.

Kullman, Colby H. "James Boswell, Compassionate Lawyer and Harsh Criminologist: A Divided Self." *Studies on Voltaire and the Eighteenth Century* 217 (1983): 199–205.

Langbein, John H. "The Criminal Trial Before the Lawyers'." *University of Chicago Law Review* 45, no. 2 (Winter 1978): 263–316.

Langford, Paul. *A Polite and Commercial People: England 1727–1783.* Oxford, 1989.

Lennox, Lady Sarah. *The Life and Letters of Lady Sarah Lennox 1745–1826.* Edited by the Countess of Ilchester and Lord Stavordale. London, 1902.

Lewis, E. H. "Are the Hackman-Reay Love-Letters Genuine?" *Modern Language Notes* 10, no. 8 (December 1895): 227–32.

Lillywhite, B. *London Coffee Houses.* London, 1963.

Linebaugh, Peter. *The London Hanged: Crime and Civil Society in the Eighteenth Century.* Cambridge, 1992.

Lockmiller, David A. *Sir William Blackstone.* Chapel Hill, N.C. 1938.

Long, O. W. "English Translations of Goethe's Werther." *Journal of English and Germanic Philology* 14 (1915): 169–203.

MacDonald, Michael. "The Secularization of Suicide in England 1660–1800," *Past and Present* 111 (1986): 50–100.

MacDonald, Michael, and Terence R. Murphy. *Sleepless Souls: Suicide in Early Modern England.* Oxford, 1990.

Marillier, Harry Currie. *A Bit of Eighteenth Century Romance. Being an Episode in the Life of Lady Mary Fitzgerald (Nee Harvey).* London, 1910.

Marsh, John. *The John Marsh Journals: The Life and Times of a Gentleman Composer (1752–1828).* Edited by Brian Robins. New York, 1998.

Martelli, George. *Jemmy Twitcher: A Life of the Fourth Earl of Sandwich 1718–1792.* London, 1962.

McCormick, E. H. *Omai: Pacific Envoy.* London, 1977.

McLynn, Frank. *Crime and Punishment in Eighteenth-Century England.* Oxford, 1991.

McManners, John. *Death and the Enlightenment.* Oxford, 1981.

Mitford, John. *Sketch of the Life and Character of Sir J. Sylvester Bart.* London, [1822].

Moorman, Mary. *William Wordsworth: A Biography.* 2 vols. Oxford, 1957, 1965.

[Mount-Edgecumb, Richard.] *Musical Reminiscences of an old Amateur.* 2d ed. London, 1827.

Musty, John. "Love and Madness." *Antiquarian Book Monthly Review* 10 (1983): 422–425.

The Newgate Calendar or Malefactors' Bloody Register. Introduced by Sandra Lee Kerman. New York, 1962.

Nicoll, Allardyce. *The Garrick Stage: Theatres and Audience in the Eighteenth Century*. Manchester, 1980.

Nocturnal Revels: or, the History of King's Place, and other Modern Nunneries. 2d ed. 2 vols. Anonymous. London, 1779.

Novak, Maximillian E. "Suicide, Murder, and Sensibility: The Case of Sir Herbert Croft's Love and Madness." In Maximillian E. Novak and Anne Mellor, *Passionate Encounters in a Time of Sensibility*. Newark and London, 1999.

Partridge, Eric, ed. *The Three Wartons: A Choice of Their Verse*. London, 1927.

Paulson, Ronald. *Hogarth*. 3 vols. Rev. ed. Cambridge, 1993.

Pettit, Henry. "The Making of Croft's Life of Young for Johnson's Lives of the Poets." *Philological Quarterly* 54 (1975): 333–41.

Phillips, Hugh. *Mid-Georgian London*. London, 1964.

Porter, Roy. *English Society in the Eighteenth Century*. London, 1982.

———. "Love, Sex, and Madness in Eighteenth-Century England." *Social Research* 53, no. 2 (Summer 1986): 211–42.

———. *Mind-Forg'd Manacles: A History of Madness from the Restoration to the Regency*, London, 1987.

Pottle, Frederick. "Boswellian Myths." *Notes and Queries*. 11 July 1925, pp. 21–22.

————. *James Boswell: The Earlier Years 1740–1769*. New York, 1966.

Radzinowicz, Leon. *History of English Criminal Law and Its Administration from 1750*. 5 vols. London, 1948–86.

Rawlings, Philip. *Drunks, Whores and Idle Apprentices: Criminal Biographies of the Eighteenth Century*. London and New York, 1992.

Rodger, N. A. M. *The Insatiable Earl: A Life of John Montagu, 4th Earl of Sandwich*. London, 1993.

Sadie, Stanley, ed. *The New Grove Dictionary of Music and Musicians*. 20 vols. London, 1980.

[Sedaine, Michel Jean.] *Rose and Colin, a Comic Opera, in one act* [in the version by Charles Dibdin]. London, 1778.

Sichel, Walter. *Emma, Lady Hamilton*. London, 1905.

Small, Helen. *Love's Madness: Medicine, the Novel, and Female Insanity 1800–1865*. Oxford, 1996.

Smith, J. T. *Nollekens and His Times*. London, 1828.

Solander, Daniel. *Collected Correspondence 1753–1782*. Edited and translated by E. Duyker and P. Tingbrand. Oslo, 1995.

Stone, Lawrence. *The Family, Sex and Marriage in England 1500–1800*. Abridged ed. London, 1979.

Taylor, John. *Records of My Life*. 2 vols. London, 1832.

Thomson, James. *The Seasons.* Edited by James Sambrook. Oxford, 1981.

Thrale, Hester. *Thraliana: The Diary of Mrs. Hester Lynch Thrale (Later Mrs. Piozzi) 1776–1809.* Edited by K. C. Balderston. 2 vols. 2d ed. Oxford, 1951.

Vaux, James Hardy. *The Memoirs of James Hardy Vaux Including His Vocabulary of the Flash Language.* Edited by Noel McLachlan. London, 1964.

Villette, John (attrib.). *The Genuine Life, Trial, and Dying Words of the Rev. James Hackman.* London, 1779.

Vivian, Frances St. Clair. "John Andre as a Young Officer," Parts 1 and 2. *Journal of the Society for Army Historical Research* 40 (1962): 24–32, 61–77.

Walker, Nigel. *Crime and Insanity in England.* Vol. 1, *The Historical Perspective.* Edinburgh, 1968.

Walpole, Horace. *Horace Walpole's Correspondence.* Edited by W. S. Lewis et al. 48 vols. New Haven, Conn. 1937–83.

———. *The Last Journals of Horace Walpole.* Edited by A. Francis Steuart. 2 vols. London, 1910.

Ward, S. G. P. *Faithful: The Story of the Durham Light Infantry.* London, 1962.

———. "The Letters of Captain Nicholas Delacherois, 9th Regiment." *Journal of the Society for Army Historical Research* 51 (1973): 5–14.

Waugh, Norah. *The Cut of Men's Clothes 1600–1900.* London, 1964.

West, Shearer. "Libertinism and the Ideology of Male Friendship in the Portraits of the Society of Dilettanti." *Eighteenth-Century Life* 16 (May 1992): 76–104.

White, L. F. W. *The Story of Gosport*. Southsea, [1949].

The Whole Proceedings upon the King's Commission of Oyer and Terminer and Gaol Delivery for the City of London and also the Gaol Delivery for the County of Middlesex. London, 1714–1800 (The Old Bailey Sessions Papers).

Wilf, Steven. "Imagining Justice: Aesthetics and Public Executions in Late Eighteenth-Century England." *Yale Journal of Law and the Humanities* 5, no. 51 (Winter 1993): 51–78.

Wu, Duncan. "Basil Montagu's Manuscripts." *Bodleian Library Record* 14 (October 1992): 246–51.

INDEX

Page numbers in *italics* refer to illustrations.